D1550891

LITERATURE

An Embattled Profession

LITERATURE

An Embattled Profession

Carl Woodring

COLUMBIA UNIVERSITY PRESS

New York

Columbia University Press

Publishers Since 1893

New York   Chichester, West Sussex

Copyright © 1999 Columbia University Press

Library of Congress Cataloging-in-Publication Data

Woodring, Carl, 1919–

   Literature : an embattled profession / Carl Woodring.

     p. cm.

   Includes bibliographical references and index.

   ISBN 0-231-11522-9 (cloth)

   1. Literature—Study and teaching (Higher)—United States.

2. Critical theory. 3. College teachers—Tenure—United States.

I. Title.

PN70.W66 1999

807'.1'173—dc21   98–49583

♾

Casebound editions of Columbia University Press books are printed on permanent and
durable acid-free paper.

Printed in the United States of America

c 10 9 8 7 6 5 4 3 2

CONTENTS

ACKNOWLEDGMENTS

Even more than my previous studies, this one has gained from professors and fellow students at Rice and Harvard and from students who taught me for nearly half a century at Columbia and Wisconsin. Carl Dawson, Theresa M. Kelley, and readers for the Columbia University Press have made considered suggestions, not all of them taken, for improving the structure, tone, and details. Elizabeth Colman, Elizabeth Forter, Joseph Kestner, Karl Kroeber, Herbert Lindenberger, Marsha Manns, Anne Mellor, James G. Nelson, Robert Patten, and Lisa Steinman have responded generously to queries. Jennifer Crewe, publisher for the humanities at the Columbia University Press, has given indispensable encouragement. The manuscript editor, Susan Heath, has caught and removed blunders with a remarkable sensitivity to the author's purposes and needs—including even the distinction in punctuation between the Ph.D. as degree and PhDs as victims. I apologize to those who have heard before—but thank those who have helped by challenging—various assertions and proposals repeated in the following pages. Even among colleagues at Columbia, they are too numerous to name.

Readers curious about the sources of bias can identify some of them in the following account: The author, after completing a B.A. and an unreadable

M.A. essay on Jonathan Swift at Rice Institute (later University), studied at Harvard under the GI Bill and under scholars biased toward the possibility of writing history; served there as graduate assistant in Renaissance and Romantic courses; and wrote a dissertation on a Victorian family of writers. Getting to teach in a university in 1948 was no problem. At the University of Wisconsin, the author first taught a course in short-story writing (i.e., reading), for students exempted from freshman composition, and a sophomore course organized by literary genres, and then various courses in nineteenth-century English literature. Like other beginning teachers there, he enjoyed support from the then rare cohort of strong women, among other gracious seniors. Gradually he became a graduate teacher—examiner, conductor of seminars, editor of dissertations—focused on Romantic authors and the 1890s, at Wisconsin and for twenty-seven years at Columbia. In the 1950s, to earn money for research in England, he helped officers of the Great Books program train lay leaders in towns of Wisconsin. He served in various national and international organizations and committees. Regarded primarily as a scholar, he frequently took the precaution of supplementing lectures with the visual aid of slides. When asked to organize the Society of Fellows in the Humanities at Columbia, with the stipulation that the Fellows would teach in the core program devoted to monumentally good books and works of similar importance in music or art, he discovered the virtue of requiring all students to undergo that sort of regimen. He lectured to freshmen for the first time at the University of Long Island, Southampton, on the evening in 1968 of the police bust at Columbia.

Academic humanists regard themselves as oppressed. They view their lot as that of legitimate heirs falsely declared by the once-beloved family to be some former foster mother's mentally deficient stepchildren. Considered economically, professors of language, literature, philosophy, music, visual arts, or any other subjects consigned to the humanities have been long underpaid in comparison with others who have undergone similarly prolonged training, and overpaid in any evaluation by society of material, intellectual, or spiritual productivity.

Few have questioned that the humanities are capable of preserving values that enhance human life. As recognized at the inception of the National Endowment for the Humanities (NEH), higher education bonds with museums, public and private libraries, historical societies, cultural foundations, private presses, and state councils of arts and letters to preserve, advance, and *produce* the humanities. The humanities in higher education combine with other public and private institutions to form a kind of urban and town companion to forests, parks, and wildlife refuges. All of them need more alert attention than they have lately had.

Standing in a turn lane, observing the fast, blinkered traffic zooming by in opposite directions, one is likely to find more ostentation than merit in the "culture wars." I propose that the practitioners of literary study in colleges and universities, who have accomplished much of national and human value, now join their detractors in allowing literature once more to have its way with the public, to permit literature to work its cure. Literature, as the inimitable product of alertness to language, alertness to signs that originated in sounds, shares with the society a need for kinds of aid neither has had recently from literature's professional students. In the ensuing chapters I argue that we professors of literature, who have ignored both public responsibility and the public as readers, should stop making it easy for the obese bureaucracies of higher education to exploit young scholars by training them for positions the system makes it impossible for them to achieve. Neither professors nor alumni, alumnae, or other voters should continue to allow managers to reduce systematically the effectiveness of higher education by reducing the proportion and the numbers of untransient full-time teachers. Professors and managers both need to acknowledge equally the essential values and the problems of securing continuity along with change through some version of the system known as tenure.

It is a concern of the present study that many humanists have attended private rituals and public ceremonies for the burial of humanism as it has descended from the Renaissance. In the tripartite division of natural sciences, social studies, and humanities, not all professors lodged in the humanities are humanistic, and not all humanists are lodged in the humanities. Linguistics housed in anthropology is regarded as a science, but at least one school of linguists could be more appropriately called exact humanists. The discipline of history remained generally humanistic for some time after it shifted attention from monarchs to the populace. More recently, uncertainty regarding representations of the past have led some annales historians to join nonhumanistic Humanists (rather than scientists of quantum mechanics) in philosophic indeterminacy. At the end of the twentieth century, Humanists by academic classification can be antihumanistic—not simply in the spirit of Osbert Sitwell's declaration in the *Who's Who* of 1933 that he was educated "during the holidays from Eton," but in soberly believing traditional humanism dead enough to make humanistic study in the 1990s a form of necrophilia. Literary study today, then, may be humanistic more by academic classification than by method or creed. Even the promise that the woman's movement would forge a link between representation and actuality—women in fiction and film, women as writers, women as victims—has partially submitted in literary study to theories of autonomous representation, the inaccessibility of the actual. This book does not, as James L. Kastely, for example, does in *Rethinking the Rhetorical Tradition*, attempt to refute postmodernism on its own terms, but agrees with Kastely that careful reading of Austen's *Persuasion* offers a better result than Paul de Man in dealing with the deceits of language.

Most of the chapters narrow the focus from humanistic endeavor in general to a subject even more vexed: academic study of literature in the United States. Details, speculations, and proposals in this "litel bok"—as Chaucer has it, "litel myn tragedye"—will concentrate on literary study, particularly on the area bulkiest in responsibilities and personnel, departments of English and American language and literature.

The central subject is literary study, with its academic and social contexts, as these have existed particularly in four-year colleges and graduate schools, undergoing change in each decade since the Civil War. The chapters address, particularly, issues that arise in institutions from which some faculty members might choose to attend annual meetings of the Modern Language Association (MLA). My experience has been primarily in research universities, public and private, and with arts and letters in independent colleges and universities of various size that encompass liberal, professional, and vocational education. I regard these, not as superior, but as distinguishable forms of education beyond what is now called, as if to avoid implied approval of the public schools, K–12. I have visited with total admiration only programs in community colleges conducting the patriotic task of remedial English.

Comprehensive, doctoral, and research universities in the twenty-first century cannot be solely devoted, as the earliest American colleges were, to the creation of public leaders. Current and future leaders of society will include a few individuals not formally educated, and perhaps a few who have majored in literature, but incalculably more from throughout the full range of postsecondary education, including the many and varied community colleges as well as the relatively few independent colleges of liberal arts. Despite the democraticization and hodgepodgification of universities, however, teachers in the humanities could through sufficient effort make sure that persons exposed to the initial stages of a broad or liberal education will be among those qualified to be national and global leaders. In those community colleges conducting something like the first two years of conventional college studies, teachers in fields of language can have the same custodial impact that the best teachers in liberal arts colleges have famously exercised, a force derived from personal devotion to works of literature and respect for individual students of personally identified promise.

In recent decades, the partitions between departments and divisions have been fractured by "studies" that extend from the humanities into social sciences or further—women's studies, Asian-American studies, African-American studies, Chicano studies, bordering studies, and folkloristic studies resurrected in envy of linguistics. As viewed by portions of the popular press, walls are crumbling from attack by these treacherous landmines. In the massive walls of elite universities, however, these fractures are as yet mere peepholes compared to other breaches.

In an institution teaching few languages, all humanistic fields may be swallowed within a Department of Communications. Often, not only in an institution small enough to combine computer science and modern languages but of late in other colleges and universities as well—often where the Librarian has become Vice President of Information Services—the heart of the humanities can be found only by diligent search within surgically created arterial bypasses. Technological advances in the era after microprocessors may confine traditional humanities to a cave cooled by the earth but in vain seeking the sun through the virtual reality piled above and around it. If so, the humanities can also heap much blame on themselves. "The humanities disciplines," it is said, "are coming to be perceived as increasingly less relevant and less necessary to modern life than other forms of knowledge" and therefore "as more expendable than other disciplines."[1]

Concern for the environment warns that expansions in population, capital, industry, and technology make immediate human need and volition inadequate determinants of action. Environmentalists have joined deconstructionists in questioning the validity of humanism at the end of the twentieth century. Fortunately, well below the Vishnuist ideal of vegetarian austerity, attentive care of ecosystems can be humanistic in name and essence. A true humanist can study the past to emulate rather than to imitate. We need not discard Erasmus because he was not an environmentalist. Humanity studies biodiversity from within the natural processes it studies. Nature and art can be opposed, but not nature and the human. Aspiration and human transgression are aspects of nature.

Conservative journalists, assuming the role of public intellectuals, have correctly observed that colleges are dispersing a previously stricter regimen into a permissive eclectic dartboard, mostly peripheral, but they are incorrect in reacting to diversity and democratized choice as a newly invented crime. Their Shakespeare was once a low-bred intruder into a tranquil academia already losing its uniformity.

Not only journalists but most who entered college after World War II view through distorting lenses college curricula and literary study before the immigration of Penguin paperbacks. Such distortion is one reason the first four chapters of this book pursue literary study and its context in the United States from Longfellow to Lacanists and Kristevists. The middle chapters trace both the intellectual disputes and the various choices professional students of literature have made to avoid addressing a general public. Literary study has not often meant the propagation of literature—has meant, that is, little propagation beyond the classroom, professional conferences, specialized journals, and each other's books. In recent decades, literary study has been an avant-garde to an era of suspicion.

History as offered in these pages is a selective record contrived after perusal and assessment of documents from a partially recoverable past. The treatment of recent and current literary study comes from personal memory and observation somewhat corrected by attention to other conscientious, fallible observers. The exponential growth in central administrations of higher education and the decrease proportionally in full-time, committed teachers is treated as demonstrable fact justly deplored by alert undergraduates.

Several chapters of this book present a jaundiced view of what emphasis on theory has so far done for literary study. Wendell Harris has shown, for example, how specific, esoteric terminology, encouraging the illusion of precision, has led to a proliferation of specific meanings for each term.[2] But claustrophilic theory was not imposed upon teachers of literature; it grew naturally from the self-enclosure that had already characterized the discipline. The eclecticism and interdisciplinarity here called for are not a skimming of theory from quantum physics and nanopsychology as a way of justifying indeterminability and destabilization in the humanities, but instead a broadening in the search for common ground in education and commonality among the educated.

The dominance of research, the opacity of terminology, and the growth of feminine and minority interests made conservative observers load their rifles; the threat of ethnic independence has encouraged them to point and fire assault weapons. Within the academic humanities, commonality, without abandoning the newly found diversity, is proposed here as a positive and not merely defensive need. Chapter 6 touches incidentally on misconceptions concerning the place and promise of technology in the humanities and on the need for adjustment among and within colleges in order to serve a student population changing demographically.

Chapter 5, "The Surround," discusses enlarged administrations, and questions of tenure, with attention particularly to the plight of educated novices and the future dependent upon them. In need of bright young teachers, we have erected factories for producing PhDs[3] and then left the product to fend for itself. Since the 1960s, embattled administrators, and more recently the tenured faculties, have paid as little serious attention to the future as the nation's representatives in Washington and in state capitols. Most faculty members have been free of rhetoric on the subject, but new attainers of the highest degree, and the students they ought to be teaching tomorrow, need action now, with or without rhetoric. To prepare universities and colleges for the twenty-first century by intellectual amputation is neither humanistic nor humane.

LITERATURE

An Embattled Profession

CHAPTER ONE

From Ancient Classics to Modern

To understand why literary study, not yet dying in a cave, has become a besieged baronial mansion, with parapets erected to make it equally fortress and prison, requires at least a cursory look into the past of the fortress, its outworks, and the surrounding territory— territory that has been a garden seemingly for meditation but with a fretwork of trenches occupied by sappers. Gibbon, in one of the less ironic sentences of his chapter 16 on Christianity, defined history as "that which undertakes to record the transactions of the past, for the instruction of future, ages." Although few now believe history capable of instructing the future, all live in a present instructed by the past, and critics ignorant of the history of literary study since the 1860s may well, in Santayana's phrase, be condemned to repeat it.

A useful beginning can be made with the world of change observed by the poet Henry Wadsworth Longfellow (1807–1882), who taught and translated at Harvard (after teaching at Bowdoin) from French, Italian, Spanish, and Portuguese; a world observed also by the poet, essayist, and physician Oliver Wendell Holmes (1809–1894), who succeeded Longfellow as Smith Professor of French and Spanish at Harvard.

Through most of the nineteenth century, "literature" included all writings that conveyed knowledge as distinguished from information. "All the branches of polite literature," commended in George Washington's will, comprised knowledge (not merely informative) of life, feelings, art, stars, birds, rocks, whatever.[1] Almanacs, instructions for beekeeping, cookbooks, and Euclid were not literature; Livy, Cicero, Aristotle, Hobbes, Hegel, Adam Smith, Malthus, Darwin, certainly Montaigne, uncertainly Diderot's and d'Alembert's *Encyclopédie*, and dubiously Sir Edward Coke's legal *Reports* and unfinished *Institutes* were literature. Literature included not only self-expression but also learning ordered and recorded as comprehensive but comprehensible—compre*hendable*—pedantry. Longfellow wrote to his father in 1837 that superintending students and instructors in four languages and hearing their recitations each month, with further responsibility for Anglo-Saxon and Swedish, would allow time for only one lecture a week in winter but in summer "two lectures per week in Belles-Lettres or Literary History."[2] "Belles-Lettres" or literary history included lectures on the middle ages, literary fame, scientific writings of the poet Francesco Redi, and "the Italian Historians, Academics, and Novellieri of the sixteenth century."[3] He did not regard lecturing to students either from notes or from a full script as an intellectual enterprise; among reasons for his resignation in 1854 he specified weariness from repeating his lectures, notably on Goethe and Dante. Students were memorably uplifted by his reading of "A Psalm of Life" at the end of a lecture, but English and American literature lay beyond his contract; he and the students had to go outside the college to hear lyceum lectures by Emerson on American subjects.

Wearying to Longfellow his lectures may have been, but they belonged to a revolution. His Dante was not only the supreme Christian humanist who depicted graphically the ways of divine justice and practiced the public service he commended but also an innovative poet who had demonstrated with intense imagination in his *Commedia*, after an implicit defense of modern languages in *De vulgari eloquentia*, the power of the Florentine dialect for moral good. If Italian literature was worth teaching, why not English, why not American?

Within the academic humanities, changes in method and content during the second half of the twentieth century have been substantial, but none have equaled the leaps in content and method throughout the second half of the nineteenth century. Greek, Latin, the Bible, and Euclid had long been basic to admission and continuance at the colleges we call—without regard to the Catholic colleges established by the Spanish and French in the New World—the "earliest": Harvard (chartered 1636), William and Mary (opened 1694), Yale (1701 as Collegiate School of Connecticut), Columbia (1754 as King's College), Brown (1765 as Rhode Island College), and Rutgers (1766 as Queen's College). We can say that the college in North America survived for three centuries with Latin, Greek, mathematics, and at least a smattering of Hebrew at its core. McGill and Toronto began with similar subjects in the 1820s.

This heritage of subjects (not yet courses) had its genesis in the Jewish and Eastern Orthodox scholars who provided the Renaissance humanists with tools for textual criticism of Greek, Hebrew, and Greek-related Latin texts both classical and Christian. These were, in Milton's words, "the languages of those people who have at any time been most industrious after wisdom," languages and stellar works in those languages necessary for "a complete and generous education" that "fits a man to perform justly, skillfully, and magnanimously all the offices, both private and public, of peace and war"—and necessary "to repair the ruins of our first parents by regaining to know God aright."[4] Like Erasmus and Sir Thomas More, the Americans would have the young take from Plutarch, Cicero, and the Bible nobility of style in speech and conduct. From Cicero they learned, besides stateliness of invective in oratory, the morality of friendship and such aspects of stoic submission to circumstances as the prudence of circumspection. From Plutarch, who was incidentally a stylist to emulate, they learned to discriminate among virtues: Plutarch's Brutus was purer in political motive than Plutarch's magnanimous Dion, but he acted in treachery; Dion, free from treachery even against a harsh tyrant, deserved censure for acting in anger over personal treatment. Classical study modified the Bible-reader's categories of angelic and diabolic.

In its earliest era Yale required mathematics only in the fourth year, but the Newtonian age demanded (in 1734) a telescope.[5] King's College, neglecting neither its Anglican purpose nor the classical tradition from Erasmus and Colet but stressing knowledge "*useful* for the Comfort, the Convenience and Elegance of Life," counted geography, history, natural philosophy, surveying, and navigation among subjects useful in a student's pursuit of happiness. Reopened after the Revolution as Columbia College, with allegiance to the Enlightenment, it appointed professors of natural history, economics, and French.[6] Opponents of change that dilutes tradition today might note the paradox here. The college established to propagate conservative Anglican doctrine, curbing the dangerously liberal influence of Harvard and Yale, introduced subjects of practicality and did so significantly earlier than London University, which was founded to provide such subjects, free of the Anglican dogma of Oxford and Cambridge foundational for the college in New York. The founders of King's College saw that neither conservation nor reaction required all four feet to remain permanently planted. Bicultural education began when Greek, Latin, and mathematics allowed a little space for discrete sciences.

The primary purpose of the earliest colleges, continued into the twentieth century in such ivied institutions as Harvard, Virginia, and William and Mary, was the education of future leaders for the improvement of government and land. Washington's will called for a university or other plan for "the youth of fortune and talents from all parts" to spread "systemic ideas through all parts of this rising Empire, thereby to do away local attachments and State prejudices . . . from our National Councils."[7] These young men of fortune were to gain knowledge in common and to form friendships in college so that members of Congress, judges, governors, and state legislators could debate amicably in the national interest.

Harvard, in keeping perhaps with its loose theology, condescended to allow students the study of French under private, subsequently licensed, tutors. At Harvard also, alertness to the new could put dents in tradition, as shown by such episodes as one that anticipates modern librarianship: when a Harvard teacher moved to Allegheny College (opened 1816), he was allowed to take first editions of works by Priestley (and books from as early as John Harvard's original gift) because Harvard had acquired later editions.

Lowly tutors, by assigning and reading daily themes, saw to it that students learned to write extemporaneously.[8] Very early on, often with the encouragement of tutors, student leaders had formed literary societies, performed plays, and produced literary magazines.[9] Undergraduate clubs, including Greek-letter fraternities, assembled libraries of magazines and current books. Students escaped into literary pursuits from the rigors of disciplined recitation. Their diaries and letters describe a life of chapel, prayer, social organizations, and adolescent mischief. Until the Civil War, students under stricter discipline than many prisons now practice unremittingly exploded in rebellion and mayhem against tutors and professors.[10]

Jefferson's vision in 1824 of students making free election among schools of ancient and modern languages, moral philosophy, law, anatomy and medicine, mathematics, natural history, and natural philosophy died in Virginia in 1831 and lay far ahead elsewhere. History did not need to be a separate program in Jefferson's scheme because the histories that had to be learned were of Greece and Rome. For all colleges of repute, Greek and Latin remained central for literature, languages, and history, with Latin crucial also for the sciences. Latin and Greek admitted inferiority only to the one subject, divinity, that neither the ordained minister as president nor his Christian board of overseers could allow a college to neglect.

With implications only gradually realized, the persuasive argument of Sir William Jones (1746–1794) that Greek, Latin, and Sanskrit descended from a common ancestral language called into question the primacy of Greek and led to an increasingly systematic study of languages, eventually to be consolidated as linguistics. By the time of Longfellow's "Indian Edda," *Hiawatha*, roughly mid-century, comparative philology competed with Greek and mathematics as a desirably strenuous mental discipline. Sufficiently stern in method, comparative philology could provide also a rationale for the broadening of study within the humanities.

In 1819 George Ticknor of Harvard, after study at Göttingen, became the first Smith Professor of French and Spanish. Chaucer and Spenser, first read in the evenings under tutelage, began to enter classrooms. Classical logic and rhetoric, earlier combined for sophistry in Latin, could now combine for sophistry in English.[11] Yet for most of the nineteenth century, in colleges purporting to train leaders, the requirements for both matriculation and curriculum remained basically classical.

When Charles W. Eliot began his campaign at Harvard in 1869 for the elective system deplored by most other college presidents, courses in Latin, Greek, Mathematics, French, elocution, and ethics, and a French history of Greece, were prescribed for freshmen. Sophomores took elocution, German, chemistry, physics, moral and economic philosophy drawn from the Enlightenment in Scotland, and late Roman history from Gibbon. They could *choose* eight or more hours a week from offerings in Anglo-Saxon, Italian, two classes (not yet organized as courses) in Greek, four in Latin, four in mathematics. After long struggle with alumni and faculty, Eliot replaced this regimen with choices among what the Rev. James McCosh, president of Princeton, called "dilettante's courses." Harvard no doubt took comfort from McCosh's complaint that Harvard required too many studies for admission: English, Greek, Latin, German, French, history, mathematics, physical science.[12] Eliot's success in introducing electives may account for suddenly increased enrollments at the more conservative Yale, Princeton, and Williams; if so, assume also that it was the abolition in 1887 of the requirement of Greek for admission that increased the numbers willing to accept Harvard's intellectual anarchy.[13] In the words of a historian of

Yale College, "The literary professor saw a chance to escape the grammarian, and the scholar glimpsed emancipation from the schoolteacher and disciplinarian."[14] Students achieved what was later called "consumer voice." The introduction of electives and the accompanying relaxation in rules and practice of discipline seem to have been followed almost everywhere by a reduction in adolescent mischief against presidents and faculties.[15] Where electives had not yet superseded an authoritarian curriculum, the rowdiness of the 1820s arose again in the 1880s and 1890s as boycotts, strikes, and demonstrations at Dartmouth, Amherst, Bowdoin, Purdue, Union at Schenectady, Missouri, and Illinois.[16] Rebellion at Amherst was led by Harlan Fiske Stone, later chief justice of the Supreme Court and trustee of Amherst.[17] Only dictators seem to realize that strict discipline is counterproductive unless accompanied by annihilation.

Philology as a scientific study of languages, the Ph.D., increased departmental autonomy, and such electives as English literature came in rapid succession. New institutions opened in what has been described as a transition from the cultivation of minds to the cultivation of useful science and practical skills: Cornell in 1868, Johns Hopkins in 1876, Clark in 1889, Stanford in 1891, Chicago in 1892.[18] Typically, Yale College became Yale University in 1887. As the century wore on, knowledge found itself no longer centered in Isocrates, Aristotle, and the Roman historians. Medieval and modern history became respectable subjects in the undergraduate curriculum. By the end of the century, fine arts and music could boast of specialized historians applying their higher degrees in classrooms. Learning dissipated in many non-European directions and into many components of physical science, natural history (mother of biological sciences), and political economy (similarly destined to undergo progressive segmentation). In the newly founded University of Chicago, the department of biology dispersed in 1893 into zoology, botany, anatomy, neurology, and physiology.[19] Euclid had come to need also Gauss and Helmholtz, and it seemed no longer of first importance that the presidents of Yale, Brown, and Columbia be ministers of the respective founding sects. Harvard, which had deliquesced from Congregationalist to Unitarian in 1806, found further dilution easy.

By the 1830s new colleges of special purpose, such as Hampden-Sidney and the city college of New York, as well as older institutions, attempted to introduce separate literary-scientific programs without lowering the prestige of traditional classics. A century later the University of Houston could open with a B.S. degree lacking the language, mathematics, and science requirements for the B.A. The prestige of the Bachelor of Arts degree survives as the ghost of Greek and Latin.

The "tradition" of requiring every student to read Shakespeare, spurred by the ubiquity of popular editions, appreciations, and theatrical successes, had a late inauguration, and it brought with it a scandalous reduction of requirements in Greek and Latin. To traditionalists of that time, only an ignorance bordering on illiteracy could have nourished the ousting of Shakespeare's moral Plutarch from the pantheon to make way for Shakespeare the unbridled playwright. The introduction of Chaucer, Spenser, Bacon, and Shakespeare in American colleges constitutes a plummeting cascade in the river of philological tradition. The admission of modern literatures into formal curricula, preceding petroleum-engineering and hotel-keeping, made the bicultural letters and sciences multicultural. Intellectual tailoring had fitted young gentlemen into Latin and Greek; a less trim population found more comfortable dress in modern literatures, and few saw Dante and Spenser as a hairshirt of penance.[20] With these changes began the decline of Plutarch's moral authority over biographers.

The three decades following the Civil War brought to higher education the state universities, the Ph.D., linguistic philology, the professionalization of disciplines, women, the teaching first of British and then of American literature, the agricultural and mechanical, and rapid steps toward elective curricula. The floodgates seemed to be open.

Victory of the North in 1865, accompanied by the petrifaction of Jim Crow, made appropriate the founding of colleges for freed slaves.

Fisk opened in 1866 and Howard opened to all qualified students in 1868; three full colleges and thirty with college work in 1915 would become seventy-seven in 1927 and more than one hundred, with generally increasing enrollments, in the 1970s, when admissions to other colleges also had become slightly more affirmative.[21] The perseverance of racial prejudice, though greatly reduced, has required a continuing maintenance of these colleges.

As an exciting departure for the humanities, the new philology, particularly etymology, provided an intellectually respectable field for research. Lovers of literature could undergo rigors of learning to obtain the Doctor of Philosophy degree imported in the 1870s, with modifications, from Europe. Johns Hopkins University opened in 1876, primarily for graduate research under two faculties, medicine and "philosophy" (comprising liberal arts and sciences).

The maturing of comparative philology, the introduction of European—particularly German—methods of specialized learning, and the emergence of English literature and language as a reputable field of study had repercussions each for the other. In departments of literature and language, philology became the dominant mode of study. Candidates for the newly crowned Ph.D. degree with English as the major field attended and contemplated etymological detail. The continuation into graduate study of translation from and into Latin, as the required evidence of discipline, gave way to analysis of linguistic forms and the tracing of English or French words and their cognates to ancestral origins.

The spirit of philological study at the doctoral level was a secularized, modern-language version of the eighteenth-century standard for admission to college: "ex tempore to read, construe and parse Tully, Virgil, or Such like common Classical Latin Authors; and to write true Latin in Prose, and to be Skill'd in making Latin verse, or at Least in the rules of Prosodia; and to read, construe and parse ordinary Greek, as in the New Testament, Isocrates, or such like, and decline the Paradigms of Greek Nouns, and Verbs."[22] The philologists did not believe that literature is an autonomous concatenation of words, free of context, but that the comprehension of literary works requires the difficult knowledge of discoverable relationships among (verbal) languages.

In the young manhood of higher education in North America, the M.A. as an earned degree was added in trepidation. In what was considered maturity, the Ph.D. spread from coast to coast. The Ph.D. created professionals in each discipline. The Modern Language Association was founded in 1883, just ahead of equivalent associations of historians and economists. Professionalization enlarged the degree of departmental autonomy; concurrently, the institution of departmental requirements for the major field of upperclassmen, amidst an increase in electives, made departments a source of recruitment for the teaching profession. This savage jungle had grown from the seed of regarding Cicero and Euclid as inadequate for learning "all the offices, both private and public, of peace and war."

That the faculties of much-altered universities remained almost altogether a male preserve assured the continuance of graduate study as a primarily male activity. The land-grant provisions of the Morrill Act of 1862 enabled states, particularly in the Mid- and Far West, to open coeducational colleges that became by the 1890s major universities, with women advancing from undergraduate through doctoral programs. Multicultural diversity began to accelerate. In the East, Oberlin included "a Female Department" in its plans of 1833 and admitted four women in 1837, but coeducation was counted among the innovations at Cornell, opened in 1868.[23] Vassar, chartered in 1861, opened in 1865, was followed in the 1870s and 1880s by other major independent colleges for women, Smith, Wellesley, Bryn Mawr, Goucher. Radcliffe, Barnard, Pembroke, and Newcomb emerged in the same years from a rib respectively of Harvard, Columbia, Brown, and Tulane. For fifteen years, from 1879, Radcliffe was the Harvard Annex for Women. The rapidity of initial steps elsewhere can be seen in statistics from the University of Michigan, with one woman in 1870 but 588 women challenging 745 men in 1898.[24] Women perturbed the young University of Chicago in 1902 by making up 52 percent of the entering class.[25] Through such conduits women began to inch toward the highest reaches of the academy. Discrimination in the society made segregated institutions slow to encourage black women into professions organized to select entrants on principles of exclusion. Humanities, however, seemed "feminine."

In English and related fields, by the middle of the twentieth century, the achievements of such women as Louise Pound of Nebraska, Fannie Ratchford of Texas, Helen White and Ruth Wallerstein of Wisconsin had reduced, if it did not silence, repetitions of such axioms as Samuel Johnson's equation of a woman preaching and a dog walking on its hind legs. Pound rebelliously concentrated on American literature and folklore. Marjorie Nicolson mentioned often her choice of Yale for graduate study because Harvard would not have permitted her to enter the stacks of Widener Library, and she frequently continued with anecdotes of seminar doors locked against her at Yale. Chairing the department of English and comparative literature at Columbia, she could limit the salaries of professors in Columbia College, but she could not make them let her teach a course there.

Even these overachievers were careful not to follow the strides of the powerful Martha Carey Thomas (1857–1935), who had progressed from a Ph.D. at Zurich in 1882 to organizer, dean, and professor of English at Bryn Mawr from 1884 until she became its president in 1894, and as suffragette took presidential control of the National Collegiate Equal Suffrage League from 1906 to 1913. Within literary study, accomplished scholars counted as black, of whatever gender, were still pulling an exceptionally heavy sack of cotton in the effort to achieve recognition.

For a Nicolson, Pound, or White success had been too hard a road for espousal of affirmative action that would give a woman privileges because she was a woman. When the head of the department at Wisconsin threatened White with dismissal from her instructorship unless she transferred her doctoral work from Radcliffe-Harvard to Wisconsin, it was not because she was a woman but because she was superior.

And when the linguist, Byronist, and poet William Ellery Leonard chased her around a circuit of desks, there was no appeal to the courts. (She outran him.) Later, in the 1960s, it was difficult for a woman to achieve tenure in the English department at Wisconsin, because White, Wallerstein, and Madeleine Doran maintained higher standards for women than for men. They could not find evidence that the requirement of higher standards imposed on them had greatly diminished anywhere in academia. Under the strict nepotism rules, a superior woman without tenure who married another English teacher, of whatever rank, had made a choice that deprived her of academic promotion. Women could provide leadership but not yet a critical mass.

Women admitted to graduate programs were expected not to demonstrate their presumed predilections for family, tender emotions, intuition, and unformularized beauty. The languages of Greek, Latin, and Anglo-Saxon had to be approached with euclidean rationality. The transformation from primarily classical to primarily modern languages had occurred without perceptible influence from women who had earned attention as novelists, poets, and editors of magazines. Those women influenced a different order of changes occurring outside academia.

Linguistic philology hampered but did not prevent the inauguration of courses that included literature in English. By 1870 sixty-three colleges had a course in English literature, usually for seniors, and twenty-six "specified some American literature" in such courses.[26] John Seely Hart taught the earliest known course in American literature at Princeton in 1872; the long-committed Americanist, Moses Coit Tyler, achieved one at Michigan in 1874. "In the four quarters of the globe," Sydney Smith had asked in 1824, "who reads an American book?"

From the beginning, graduate studies culminating in the Ph.D. had the professional aim of scholarship alone, while "literature" was becoming only those writings lacking any hint of the professional. Toward the end of the nineteenth century, publishers' lists in Great Britain and North America began to segregate fiction, drama, poetry, and personal essays under the heading *Belles Lettres*. The personal essay was exactly what graduate study could not be. Fewer and fewer personal essays achieved the status of bound collections; in the United States the personal essay was on its way to a specialty of the *New Yorker* magazine. In *Harper's*, the *Atlantic*, and quarterlies, personal essays surrendered to articles, either baldly expository or arguing from empirical accumulations of fact. Even the little magazines took their purpose of opposing the general culture of market and commodity too seriously to welcome personal essays. Casual peculiarity had lost value when "American culture itself became a purchasable commodity."[27]

In the curriculum of English departments, although essays had not been banished from specialized anthologies of seventeenth-century or nineteenth-century literature, by 1940 Bacon, Hazlitt, "Elia," and Stevenson were on the brink of exclusion from introductory courses in composition. For the following three decades, "literature" as taught in English departments was scarcely distinguishable from "belles lettres," but the departments of that era (and after) wished to convince others that freshman composition courses served the expository needs of the social and natural sciences.

Humane naturalists such as Rachel Carson, in succession to John Muir, occasionally illuminated in language of imagination and feeling the otherwise expository, often statistical, articles that served as models of organized thought in textbooks of composition. Examples of exposition for freshmen excluded such social critics of flair as Lewis Mumford and even the environmental essayist, drama critic, and professor of literature, Joseph Wood Krutch. Senior professors had allowed the contraction to empirical exposition for three reasons: a sense of obligation to less literary departments, an Imagistic-experiential preference for particulars over generalization, and indifference toward freshman composition. For graduate students, literature was something one learned, composition was something one taught.

Etymology endured as a graduate subject. Well into the 1920s the "oral" examination for the Ph.D. in English at reputable universities had required a blackboard on which the candidate could draw the tree of cognates for words of Germanic origin in a sentence or line of Chaucer, Shakespeare, Spenser, Bacon, or Milton—cognates in languages including Old Norse, Old High German, and the largely hypothetical Gothic. Chaucer's "Nat greveth us youre glorie and youre honour" called for a similar tree that included old and modern French as well as Latin. The inclusion of Sanskrit was generally left to more serious students of language than the candidate who was about to embark upon, or had successfully completed, a doctoral dissertation concerned with a work or works of literature in English.

Procedures in graduate study were more etymologically stringent than those in college courses, but at Harvard in the 1920s four years of English for undergraduates meant Shakespeare, Chaucer, Spenser, and Bacon (at Columbia, Milton instead of Bacon), in whose behalf the lecturer provided etymological cognates for each significant word in the fifty pages or so that could be analyzed in the nine months of one academic year. And then arrived the sophomore survey of English literature from *Beowulf* to a date somewhat near that of the anthology. For upperclassmen more diffuse courses, surveying literary developments and achievements in general or by genre or during particular periods, offered increasingly a wealth of choice lamented by philologists.

Graduate students found pleasure in turning from dry memorization of Old Norse to the humanistic insight that *alms* is *eleemosynary* progressively shortened in casual speech (with Chaucer's *almesse* intermediate), or that *holy child* and *silly brat* are terms so related through *selig* and Old Irish for a cloak as to be twins all but identical. Here again superior pleasure came from knowing the linguistic process involved: the innocent are among the blessed because God cares for idiots; ergo, *sely* becomes, because it includes, *silly*. There was high fun in realizing that knowledge of linguistic change enabled George Lyman Kittredge to discover in the seafaring ballad of the "Amphord Wright" a lament for the sunken ship *Amphitrite*. Etymology survives in collegiate dictionaries available in every bookstore with as many books as T-shirts, and not merely as information but because pleasure accompanies learning that the word *precocious* referred first to early ripening food, from *coquere*, to cook.

There was much besides derivation of words to be learned: competing explanations of changes in spelling, changing rules of grammar, changes since Quintilian in devices of rhetoric, common and uncommon figures of speech (e.g., epanalepsis), and figures of thought (synecdoche, irony), the evolution of genres, changing rules and practices of versification (meter, stanzaic patterns), and dates, dates, dates—birth, death, and changes of status of major authors—When was Rabelais in Rome?—monarchs, dynasties, revolutions, gunpowder plots, institutional and theological reformations.

Conditions of preparation and defense were not altogether punitive. The earliest dissertations from the English department at the University of Wisconsin included three on living authors, Tennyson, Browning, and Oliver Wendell Holmes—none of the three expected to make further contributions of significance, but alive. As no burden from past doctorates imposed restrictions, dissertations in literature could be broad enough to encourage piquant illustration without any requirement of proof or conclusive demonstration: The Farmer in English Literature from *Piers Plowman* to Thomas Hardy; Pastoral Metaphors in English Poetry; Influence of the Ablative Absolute on Grammatical Constructions in English Drama.

The underlying principle of originality required each candidate to propose a topic nobody else had adequately undertaken. Once the dissertation on parsons appeared in bibliographies, a second work on the same subject could not be thought original, but greater attention to detail could justify a doctoral study of the parson in fifteenth-century verse and subsequent studies of the parson in sixteenth-century drama, eighteenth-century fiction, and all the other pigeonholes from which parsons could be extracted. A doctoral candidate in comparative literature, in English, or in German could be assigned, as dissertation topic, views of Goethe expressed in English literature of the nineteenth century. Subsequent candidates could examine in fuller detail Goethe in English literature of the first half of the century, the second half, then 1832 (Goethe's death) to 1855 (biography by G. H. Lewes). The end of this line is "Views of Goethe in English-Language Studies of Thomas Mann, 1935–1955." Meanwhile, obviously enough, the requirement of originality forced every university to make available bibliographic lists of previous domestic and foreign dissertations, articles in scholarly journals, and recent books. A sense of originality that required no bibliographic search lay far ahead.

A dissertation on the parson in all of English literature needed only to classify the views discovered and quoted. When the parson is studied in literature of a limited period, fictional and poetic representations were seen to need comparison and contrast with data concerning actual parsons in surviving documents or with summaries of the evidence by historians who had consulted factual documents. If the sharpest students of 1880–1910 were expected to make linguistic discoveries and the second sharpest to make etymological analyses of the language in particular literary works, others could be encouraged to place the works of a major writer within biographical or social contexts. A candidate thought unimaginative could be allowed to offer as dissertation an annotated bibliographic list only if accompanied by an introduction containing intellectual analysis. Philological knowledge, or information, was required of all; a candidate who quoted the *Encyclopædia Britannica* should know how to spell it, and why.

The Ph.D. degree in North America proclaimed mastery of research; it prescribed training in approved methods for research in a particular field. To emulate the precision of natural sciences, evidences of discipline had to be maintained: for social studies, statistics; for the humanities, language. The author of a dissertation on Samuel Johnson's religious views had undergone training for linguistic analysis before individual research into Anglican doctrine and competing sects in eighteenth-century England—and had reached a concluding generalization believed to be original.

Even when not subversive of discipline by including living authors, the doctoral dissertation was a liberalizing force within graduate programs in the humanities. In theory, the dissertation came from a man—and why should a theory not assume that it came in that period from a *man*—so trained as to bring new knowledge to all other students and professors of either (a) sciences or (b) humanities. In 1930 it could be assumed of the Ph.D. degree that "persons who have had a genuine university education will emerge with disciplined minds, well stored with knowledge, possessing a critical, not a pedantic edge," and that "such persons may thereafter for the most part be safely left to their own devices."28

The land of the free left it to Russia and other retrograde nations to require the nailing of theses to an oak door for defense in a public square, but in American universities professors from outside the candidate's department judged the work, and faculty and students from other fields were invited by announcement of place and time to listen or to challenge. More to the point, they were expected to find that the candidate had made both the subject and the findings of the widest interest the subject could support.

The requirement in some universities that a dissertation be published before the degree was awarded, and in most that the examiners judged the dissertation to be publishable, came in part from desire within the academy to reach a wider audience. This particular test of quality could be settled by a candidate possessing the funds to subsidize publication, but a dissertation committee could require that the topic, however narrow, be presented in language accessible to the widest audience capable of interest in its addition to knowledge. The presence of judges from outside the candidate's specialty not only kept a department from falling below the standards of fellow departments but also encouraged the virtue of accessibility. (Of late, the arrangement may lead to a transfer of esoteric language into an external judge's own department.)

In theory, the holder of a doctorate had learned methods of research applicable in any field of scholarship. The title of Doctor called upon the medieval tradition of honoring minds so superior they could master and teach any subject: initially, the Doctors of the Latin Church, St. Ambrose, St. Augustine, St. Gregory the Great, and St. Jerome. The model for "Doctor" is an Aristotle or Pascal.

Compartmentalization early on led from the original recognition of universal wisdom to earned doctorates in law and in divinity (twelfth century) and in medicine (fourteenth century). By the eighteenth century, "the Age of Reason," a doctorate could be earned in almost any subject taught in colleges. A sense of honoring wisdom remained, and the intellectual discrepancy between medical theory and practice by physicians in England and Scotland led the College of Surgeons to emphasize the distinction between surgeons ("Mr.") and physicians ("Dr."). A similar suspicion of "Dr." could have spread further without great harm. In descent from St. Augustine, the honorary doctorate has progressively passed to Samuel Johnson, Thomas Alva Edison, prominent actresses, and a donor who adds substantially to the endowment of a university.

The aura of the "highest degree" survived into the 1940s. James B. Conant, as president of Harvard, conferred by formula such lesser degrees as bachelor, master, engineering, law, and medicine. Then as Dr. Conant he invited all candidates for the degree of doctor of philosophy who might (voluntarily) be present, to gather near him for welcoming into the fellowship of scholars. The conferring without other formula of that "highest degree" implied that the recipients, even if there was something they did not know, could learn anything needful without further institutional training. The procedure implied, what was then still practiced, that a person could earn only one "highest degree." Reality, probably tinctured with greed, soon led universities to confer successively on one person an indeterminate number of doctoral degrees in jurisprudence, law, English, comparative literature, molecular biology, social work, whatever.

My Harvard diploma of MDCCCCXXXXVIIII, signed by Jacobus Bryant Conant, elevated me "ad gradum Philosophiae Doctoris" because of my diligent study of Philologia, specifically Philologia Anglica, but the linguistic requirements had shrunk to Old English and translation in mild tests from Latin, German, and French, with little expectation that the average recipient would be able to read the diploma.

Intellectual respectability had come to require the principle that any high school graduate could understand grammatical usage in works subsequent to the Renaissance; a graduate in English needed therefore to learn what changes had occurred in the language up to and including Milton. Spenser required linguistic analysis; Tennyson hardly at all. Old English and the history of the language, from before the earliest documents through the Renaissance, remained staples of graduate study in English. In most universities *Beowulf* was taught, not as a literary composition but as a wordhoard, a storage bin of Anglo-Saxon linguistic traits.

Most graduate schools grudgingly allowed dissertations on living authors, but the rule of linguistic analysis created a scale of respectability. *Beowulf* conferred the greatest dignity; Gower (d. 1408) was sufficiently forbidding; Henry James was safely dead and usefully ironic; the living Forster and Faulkner were tainted possibilities. At Johns Hopkins a dissertation could be written on Wordsworth, born in 1770, but not one on an author as recent as Keats, born in 1795. About 1955 Merritt Y. Hughes, Miltonist, could question the respectability of writing on the illiterate Faulkner. The sense that recent centuries provided only unscholarly subjects, absent at the origin of the Ph.D. in literature, had reached arteriosclerosis within the division of humanities in many graduate schools. The professor who taught the history of the English language saw little reason for lecturing on changes after 1660 (or 1674), but he or the unlikely she could foresee disastrous decline elsewhere in the department. As the number of dissertations increased, it became convenient for the professors of literature to grant that Gibbon and Samuel Johnson constructed sentences in ways not common after 1800, and who could deny that Carlyle's way with language in *Sartor Resartus* (1833–1834) invited analysis?

From its inception as a degree for researchers, the Ph.D. had evoked dissent from committed teachers. Near the turn of the century the department of English at Columbia University, besides a forced return of comparative literature, held in uneasy harness three divisions: philology, literature, and rhetoric, later to be called composition. The rebels who argued for the study of literature, not language, insisted on values. If the sciences claimed to be value free, let it be so; literature belonged to a universe of values. Rebels who had earned the philological Ph.D. now declared that course of study free equally of values and of interest. The presence of such rebels at Columbia and elsewhere probably accounts in part for the discrepancy early on between linguistic discipline and the humane laxness of dissertations on broad subjects. Leonard, at Wisconsin, was Anglo-Saxonist, poet, and Byronist. World War I created a patriotic interest in things American, including literature. It could now be studied professionally without apology.

The strength that proponents of value had contrived to collect at the turn of the century fell far short of toppling emphasis on language. The sciences had replaced reading with finding out and doing; the need of scientists for time to conduct experiments soon gave results from research precedence over teaching, priority over acclaim from students for making even *Pilgrim's Progress* interesting. Teachers who had hoped to revive pleasure in intrinsic study of individual works would soon be driven to achieve the status of researcher by immersing works into contexts. The study of contexts would be, they thought, not linguistic study, but literary.

CHAPTER TWO

From Language to Context

As decades rolled by, attention to literature in the stead of language and rhetoric increased. That the twentieth century began with what William R. Everdell in *The First Moderns* (1997) calls the discovery of discontinuities had no effect in departments that were studying the past. Virginia Woolf's date for the transformation of human nature, December 1910, is a bit early for intellectual transformation within English departments, but the entrance of veterans from World War I and the advance of modernism in literature and other arts accompanied a desertion of allegiance to language in favor of literature and its social contexts.

The emphasis on context in literary study of the 1930s was less revolution than evolution, but reformation in the 1920s and 1930s is much more significant than younger scholars today can imagine. In a history of literary criticism for *Daedalus* in 1997, Catherine Gallagher can declare, "Before the New Criticism, the primary object of scholarship was language"; for her, the New Critics set about to overthrow a study of literature that had as its purpose knowledge "about the history and structure of the language."[1] Refutation of the doctrine that literary scholarship began and ended in language had been solidly accomplished in the 1930s. Most professors of English in the 1930s believed that the mechanics of language, among the many factors serving the creation of a work of literature, performed a relatively minor and relatively uninteresting role. They retained language as a requirement for graduate study, not for teaching, research, or publication. Like their predecessors who had emphasized language, they continued to believe that teachers of composition, rhetoric, and literature could instill in receptive students clarity of thought, vigor of expression, pursuit of truth (pursuit, not possession, on the paradigm of "pursuit of happiness"), and recognition of beauty. They believed in the possibilities of knowledge as distinct from information.

A handbook for cramming by Professor William B. Otis of the College of the City of New York with Morriss H. Needleman, *A Survey-History of English Literature* (1938), of 580 pages (followed by 20 pages, as appendix in smaller type, on writers of the twentieth century), well represents the era with its plethora of authors, titles, dates, characteristics, and, of style, "suggested merits" and "suggested defects" documented from critics of authority.

Two quotations from Otis and Needleman can suggest accurately enough what would be expected on a doctor's oral of the 1940s:

John Marston, *The Metamorphosis of Pygmalion's Image: And Certain Satires* (1598). Erotic, coarse, virulent, turgescently-worded satirical poem. Six-line stanzas, in same meter as Shakespeare's *Venus and Adonis*. Ordered burned by Archbishop Whitgift.

And under "The Triumph of Neo-Classicism. The Beginnings of Journalism. a) The Newspaper":

The first regular English paper was Nathaniel Butler's *The Weekly News* (1622–1641). During the Civil War many courants, diurnals, and news-sheets were issued. Prominent were Roger L'Estrange's *The Intelligencer* (1663); *The London Gazette* (1666), the only serious attempt at journalism during the seventeenth century, one controlled by the Under-Secretary of State.

"a) The Newspaper" is followed by "b) The Periodical." A candidate expecting to pass the doctor's oral with distinction would know that a more authoritative historian than Otis had designated as the first English newspaper Thomas Archer and Nicholas Bourne's *A Current of General News*, registered at the Stationers' Office May 18, 1822.

A literary work was thought to have characteristics discoverably influenced by the author's family, neighborhood, education, truant reading, pals, correspondents, rivals, cruel employers, and subjection to social, political, and religious streams flowing or trickling into the community. The scholar sought particulars: what mansions, hovels, gardens, forests, beggars, and corpses had the author seen? What scientific theories, news stories, and editorials were available to be read? The scholar utilized intensive training in literary history and genres to examine the heritage if not the burden of the past, but thought that the language of a local school or newspaper also might speak through great authors. Contextual research might lead to such notable discoveries as Madeleine Stern's that Lousia May Alcott, author of *Little Women*, had pseudonymously published lurid tales, but the significant claim being made for contextual research was that it aided comprehension and interpretation not only of sentences and paragraphs but of literary works as constructed entities. Some holders of graduate degrees in English, drilled in data, did not realize that the claim was being made.

The search for facts, lacking the fire of religious faith, carried with it a perpetual threat of dullness. Scholars piled fact on fact with the assumption that some sage would eventually stand atop the pile and proclaim a critical judgment. Needles in the haystack were errors that might or might not emerge. Quests for certainty could conceal larger errors. The scholarly author of a large book might conclude that because opium addicts in a Los Angeles jail couldn't dream a "Kubla Khan" Coleridge couldn't either. When biographers knew that Dorothy Wordsworth accompanied her brother to Calais in 1802 but did not know that he had sired a daughter in France, the anthology of English Romantic poetry standard for half a century annotated "Dear Child!

dear Girl! that walkest with me here" as the poet's sister, even though that annotation made nonsense of the poem. Knowledge that Dorothy was present hindered interpretation. Similarly, as long as Byron's editors were unaware of his attachment to the chorister Edleston, their annotations made hash of the lines, "There be none of Beauty's daughters / With a magic like thee." As it would have been unpalatable to believe the lyric addressed to a girl of sweet voice issuing from an ugly face, critics thought that the "none" illustrated Byron's careless syntax—until scholarship pointed to Edleston. Facts nevertheless exist, despite current denials, for recognition and interpretation, as in the dictionary example unavailable in the 1930s, "space travel is now a fact."

Insistence at a later time that objectivity is impossible because the observer is always present in the perception represents increased alertness to generalization; scholars of the 1930s attentive to particulars, immersed in history, achieved more frequently than critics in an era of generalizing theory intoxication by something other than the zeitgeist. Although recognizing the difficulty of mitigating the effects of their own cultural environment and prejudices, they had too little interest in abstract theory to believe effective mitigation impossible. Their tendencies toward empirical positivism included observable restraints. Embarrassing personal and social questions to be asked by later undergraduates were not asked in classrooms of the thirties; perhaps very little then said by the teacher of literature aroused sophomores' curiosity.

As infrequently as the Victorian scientists called positivists (meaning slaves to Comte, or know-nothings) did the literary scholars of the thirties claim to be positive. Without grasping the implications of Jevons's prediction that "the Reign of Law will prove to be an unverified hypothesis, the Uniformity of Nature an ambiguous expression, the certainty of our scientific inferences to a great extent a delusion," T. H. Huxley came to realize that the reality studied by scientists was "a symbolical language, by the aid of which Nature can be interpreted in terms apprehensible to our intellects."[2] Most of the literary scholars had read

Huxley and knew fiction to be the representation of representation. No deep chasm there. They knew that "facts" had to be filtered and interpreted. But awareness that what happened in the French Revolution would always be uncertain did not for them mean that *War and Peace* could be studied only as language.

They gave attention to genre and convention. Each work studied was a unique exemplar of the way genre changes like dough under the kneading fingers of context. Distinctions between text and context became blurred when they were not successfully annihilated. Each work studied had swallowed its surroundings. Everything external uncovered by the scholar but unabsorbed in the work being studied was to be put aside, awaiting the scholar's encounter with a work more susceptible to what had been uncovered. The scholar interpreted, not "text" in a later restricted sense but a work, which included, however transformed, what it had absorbed.

A scholar thus became expert in certain aspects of certain periods, expert in a context and in both "major" and "minor" literary works within that context. Inevitably the search led to the identification of works as more absorptive of that particular scholar's "context" than other scholars thought the works to be. The enterprise required both the assertor and dissenters to describe and define the text-in-context. For such an enterprise John Livingston Lowes's *The Road to Xanadu*, pursuing Coleridge's chain reading from each book to others cited in that book, came to seem exemplary. Focus upon texts transmitted in print was sufficiently intense for E. E. Stoll to startle his colleagues by insisting that Shakespeare should be read as theater.

For these scholars, sociologists had useful perceptions, not universalizing theories usable as weapons against trust in language. Most scholars of the thirties practiced positivistic explorations from a base in Romantic idealism, with little acknowledgment of Romantic skepticism. When all else was accounted for, there remained genius, inspiration from within and from birth, as distinguished by Coleridge and other Romantics from talent. A scholar devoted to Pope might detest

Shelley and Turner and Schumann but would accept evidence on the page that Shakespeare was a genius.

With all their attention to material context, literary scholars of the 1930s come equally near deserving the sobriquet of positivists by their faith in intention. With few exceptions, they accepted as usable for interpretation not only declarations of intention by an approved author but also what self-declared spokespersons for a period or "school" declared as the characteristics distinguishing them from the purposes and failures of their immediate predecessors. They studied to learn what Aristotle, Horace, Longinus, Sidney, Boileau, Hegel or the Schlegels, Wordsworth, Coleridge, Shelley, Arnold, and Pater said, and what each intended to say.

Consider, though, Richard Wollheim's argument in *Art and Its Objects*—directed in 1968 against Croce—that a work of art exists as such only if the person or persons initially responsible for its availability intended it to be taken as a work of art. A bit of driftwood or a toilet seat is not art until somebody presents it as art and some other person of authority within the institutions of that art accepts the denomination. Driftwood cannot intend to be art, sunbathers have not perceived it as art, but one individual has made it art by intending it to be. A dealer has declared its aesthetic and monetary value before an auctioneer will care to test the market. Next question? Scholars of the thirties asked next what kind of a poem the poet intended it to be. What kind of audience did the author expect, or have reason to expect, and what could the author of a given word in context have anticipated that the audience would make of that word? How would the expected audience construe the word and how would they *feel* it? How far could the work be shown to be without precedent? And why?

The assumption that a created work communicated to others meanings ideally discoverable by severe research and chance encounter, thereby positing a means of contact between work and reader, encouraged in published essays emphasis on a single aspect of the relationship, whether text, author, or audience. Without scrupulous analytic reading, interpretations were stable enough to make the slightest demurral widely mentioned. An adventurous anthology, in a footnote of one sentence stretching beyond fact, could convey what Milton's sonnet on the massacre in Piemont meant. It was hard to rock a boat that had long been securely aground. No place was found for that profusion of interpretive notes to come in the Norton anthologies. The reason for caution has been aptly defined: "It is as though poetic meaning and expression were intransitive; that is, we can know that a poem means, and means vividly and memorably, but we cannot say precisely what a poem means."3 Guys of the thirties—including those famous women—crossed in humility the threshold from external particulars to nebulous interior. Lytton Strachey on eminent Victorians served as example of what to avoid.

The assumption of communication with an audience carried with it inevitably a degree of indeterminacy. Scholars paid little attention to the concept of reader response expressed in John Erskine's insistence that a line in one of Shakespeare's plays or in Milton's *Paradise Lost*, as well as each work as a whole, could have no certain meaning but varied with every audience. Audiences were more important than an author's intentions, however, in the tacit agreement to teach works meeting Samuel Johnson's criterion for significance: what has pleased many and pleased long. Their canon had been constructed by audiences, had been determined by reception as encouraged through appraisal. Even a work that had failed to rise immediately as cream deserved certification by its survival while a succession of tasters had ladled whole seas of liquid from the vat to oblivion.

Although W. W. Greg had not yet urged the greater reliability of the earliest text of a work, on the theory of deterioration in subsequent reprintings, many American scholars of the thirties became uneasy over the principle of granting highest authority to the latest text seen by the author—because that might not be the version approved by generations of readers. Few doubted, for example, that Leigh Hunt might have modified Keats's "La Belle Dame sans Merci" into the version beginning "Ah, what can ail thee, wretched wight" instead of the "O what can ail thee, knight at arms" of the manuscripts, but a century of editors and critics had made Hunt's version the one responsible for the poem's reputation. These professors were teaching the history of English literature, which to a notable degree was a history of reception. Existence of a canon for teaching had resulted from a collaboration of creation and reception. From Keats, again, in "The Eve of St. Agnes" it was thought unlikely that the poet consented to the omission of the stanza on delicious pleasures in Madeline's dream, but the received version, without the stanza, was the version known, approved, and to be transmitted.

Not from the introduction of the Ph.D. until the 1930s, and in no period after, did the teaching in English departments of graduate students and undergraduates employ methods so nearly the same. It can also be said for the naive disorder of the 1930s, employing relativity in practice rather than in theory, that scholars generally—there were several notable exceptions—avoided the application of a prevailing theory to bury individuality under a general law.

College teachers of the 1930s, elevated into graduate faculties in the 1940s, were emboldened to teach doctoral candidates the literary and contextual aspects of works they lived with instead of linguistic principles from their own training. They were not ready to offer options excluding Old English, but despite a residue of fear that they were introducing lower standards of intellectual discipline, they collectively spared the next generation of doctoral candidates such triumphs of rote memory as they had been required to accomplish.

Trained in etymology, these college teachers of English literature in the 1930s rejoiced in the novelty of relating works of literature to their material contexts. They could not miss the materiality all around them in the shape of poverty, labor "unrest," foreclosures, and bankruptcies. Professorial experience of near poverty was reinforced with each month's low wage for teaching. At the University of Wisconsin the tenured faculty voted to accept half pay to avoid the alternative of eliminating all assistant professors, teaching assistants, lecturers, and other teaching positions not bearing tenure.[4] Long before *Puritan* had become a term of opprobrium, all authors of note agreed that the fuel of American society was money; now professors joined poets from Emerson to Pound and Eliot in regarding money as an inadequate medium for the reduction of individuated isolation.

Suddenly, in sizable intellectual circles in and out of the universities, proposals for the redistribution of wealth vied with schemes for equalization. Professors in the humanities had less temptation than sociologists and political scientists to declare approval of socialist nations or systems, but sympathy for economic intervention or control by government spread year by year. If professors in the humanities did not in large numbers vote for the Socialist candidate for president, Norman Thomas, they read enthusiastically the *Nation*, the *New Republic*, and the *Partisan Review*, if not the *New Masses*. Half the intellectuals in large cities, in and out of universities, believed in the intellectual sanctity of Leon Trotsky.

If students could not afford to buy Dos Passos's *U.S.A.* or Steinbeck's *The Grapes of Wrath*, they could be encouraged to borrow both from a public or college library. They could be enlightened by exposure to Clifford Odets's *Waiting for Lefty*. The time for Richard Wright's *Native Son* lay ahead.

If you scratched a teacher of literature in those years, even the staidest, you would almost certainly have found a political liberal. None doubted that Democrats believed in people, Republicans in property. Nevertheless, the study and description of literary works in biographical, social, and political context flourished with little direct input from views that the teacher could not find explicit on the page.

They were made more timid than they otherwise would have been by the way they understood the responsibility to be *just* as requiring an objectivity rationally achieved. Scholars as well as teaching assistants tended to underassign antiliberal works, but along with rhetorical devices and intricacies of structure they taught only what they believed clearly present in the work at hand. Liberation from etymology made the detached study of contexts, or a conscientious attempt at detachment, exciting enough. Examination today of dissertations of the 1930s on literary subjects reveals little change from previous, more language-minded decades in degree of difference between the political or social bias of the doctoral candidate and the bias evident in the literature studied. And Jack London was almost as unlikely a subject for study as J. P. Marquand. Some of the neutrality of method would have come from the fear of being fired or expelled, but most came from sharing the myth of scientific detachment. The context of literature was a world of searchable if not absolutely certain fact. Beyond fact, the scholar sought truth.

The canon within English literature included everything written in the British Isles with intelligence and feeling before 1901. The range of lesser authors to be studied could be influenced effectively only by anthologists, but the range available for dissertations can be extrapolated from a few chapter titles in *The Literature of the Victorian Era* (1910) by Hugh Walker: Theology, Philosophy, The German Influence, Science, Minor Poets ("The Interregnum" and later), History and Biography, Miscellaneous Prose, and chapters on "developments" in fiction and poetry.

The canon of major authors had remained almost stable well into the 1930s, on Johnson's receptionist principle of pleasing many and long. A few notable elevations had occurred. Attention by Edmund Gosse and H. J. C. Grierson to John Donne enabled T. S. Eliot to promote Donne into a much higher place in the canon than he had previously occupied. Edmund Blunden in 1921 and J. W. Tibble in 1935 secured for John Clare the rung previously shared by Robert Bloomfield, Henry Kirk White, and William Motherwell. Robert Bridges astounded serious readers when he published in 1918 poems by his friend Gerard Manley Hopkins. It required a subsequent change in poetic taste to make Hopkins a major figure. Christopher Smart no longer seemed to belong among minor, mad, and buried poets when his *Jubilate Agno* was rescued in 1939. In American studies the discovery of Edward Taylor's manuscripts revealed a major Puritan; Emily Dickinson and Herman Melville rose above Whittier and Howells.

As a general rule only the discovery of a neglected manuscript could crown with success a critic's efforts to claim majesty for an author left by tradition among the average specimens of a period or style. Although John Crowe Ransom could declare Edna St. Vincent Millay blind to her era because she lacked a taste for Donne, stability from Shakespeare to Arnold was such that neither New Critics nor deconstructionists would substantially disturb that upper canon. In the 1950s Northrop Frye's single-handed hoist of William Blake academically out of the eighteenth century, where Blake was little honored, into the next period, increasing the Great Romantic Five to Six, was the accomplishment of a titan.

The canon was extended chronologically, first in dissertations, then in surveys, and finally in periodization. In the 1820s the academy believed that books written in modern languages were self-explanatory; in the 1920s contemporary literature was thought to be either beneath explanation or (*The Waste Land*, *Ulysses*) beyond it. But what else, besides composition, were PhDs who had written on contemporary authors to teach? They had survived etymological training; they had proved their originality in dissertations on authors their seniors had not read until this duress; how could they be denied courses in the field where they had unique authority? Their courses produced an anomaly that has remained: twentieth-century literature of Britain joined to that not of Canada but of the United States, a twain that seldom meets in courses confined to earlier centuries.

Occasionally in department meetings or even in discussions concerned only with the graduate program, a worrier would ask if literary study could not be made more professional by requiring courses in the philosophy of literature and the history of literary theory. If not everywhere, then typically, colleagues answered that the requirements already omitted so much important literature that the introduction of a single course in literary criticism would dislodge works more essential to mastery of literature, the reason for departmental existence. Courses in theories of literature and history of criticism were much more likely where comparative literature existed as a separate department.

Along the way, writers once prized as stylists had lost prestige. Sir Thomas Browne's conscious quaintness could no longer escape its own seventeenth century. Students ceased to encounter Bacon's beginnings: "Suspicions amongst thoughts are like bats among birds, they ever fly by twilight"; "He that hath wife and children hath given hostages to fortune; for they are impediments to great enterprises, either of virtue or mischief." Charles Lamb, as clear-eyed and candid as any writer in the language but misread as sentimental, sank with other conscious stylists. Of the comic poets loved by the Victorians, only those treasured for the psychology of nonsense, Edward Lear and Lewis Carroll, survived.

By the thirties, speech was only rarely taught in English departments, and oratory had dropped out of the canon. The few senior teachers of rhetoric had earned a Ph.D., likely enough, with a dissertation on orations, extracted usually from Greek or American oratory or, for some, from the French Revolution, perhaps in its relation to the oratory of Milton's day in England. It was not thought necessary, however, to have pursued a higher degree in order to teach clarity and force of expression to young persons entering college. Basic writing was not thought to need the full trinity of previous centuries: clarity, force, and elegance.

In transition, in a university with a graduate-degreed professor of rhetoric surviving as a relict, the underlings who taught composition had that expert as master. When the masters of rhetoric retired for home or grave, a replacement of lower rank and salary took over. Thereafter, candidates for the chair of rhetoric at Harvard were poets. The decline of rhetoric as doctoral subject led to lower standards for composition. In the decay of rhetoric lay the seeds of the perceived inferiority of full-time teachers of composition, including the head of that program likely to be the dominant power in the graduate career of teaching assistants. The perception of inferiority has continued because university administrations prize publication of a kind the director of composition has no opportunity to attain.

Masters of rhetoric ceased to be needed, because freshman composition became the one course in English departments designed to serve other interests than the student's and the department's. Persuasion, except in principled literary criticism, came to seem a dishonest way of writing. Some composition classes illustrated dishonest use of language in samples of persuasive commercial advertising. Disinterested exposition required only clarity and precision. Imagination belonged in courses of English or American literature for upperclassmen. Most freshmen would need later to write clear papers for professors of history, sociology, science, business. Freshman composition served the academic community; literature served the individual student; increasingly, the teaching of literature served itself.

So Demosthenes was no longer one of the reasons for learning Greek. Other reasons faded as well. One year of Greek seemed worthless, and fewer and fewer undergraduates arrived with anything to build on. Graduate students no longer had the scaffold for constructing etymologies. As ancient Greek first and next Old Norse and Old High German and then Latin came to seem empty exercises for graduate students in the humanities, the languages remaining for humanistic discipline were modern French and German. These were not only languages of great literature but also languages of scholarship on humanistic subjects, as Italian and Spanish only intermittently were. Never mind that the *Encyclopedia Britannica* had declined to a level of scholarship well below that of encyclopedias in Spanish and Italian; journals of current scholarship in European literature came to university libraries from France and Germany. A doctoral candidate in English had to be prepared for (or against) an article in German comparing Keats and Hölderlin in the *Journal of English and Germanic Philology*. Patriotic prejudice in the wake of two massive wars would leave German a starved subject in American public schools and undernourished for graduate study; Nazi rule made German scholarship suspect. French rose by default. Latin survived for discipline in a few institutions, but no holder of a Ph.D. in English was any longer qualified by that degree to teach the terminology of medicine.

Meanwhile, emphasis on division into specialized subjects authorized professorial scorn for the institutions that subordinated academic subjects to theory, method, and practice in teaching, the institutions that rose steadily from "normal school" for elementary teachers into "teachers' college" for all public schools and on (in parallel with colleges of agriculture and engineering) to "state university." Professors of university subjects continued to ignore these "educators" and their direction of the public school system in each state. As parents of children in the middle grades, aloof professors suffered personal pain, but they were deacons of society looking away while the educators as young harlots seduced the state legislatures. Literary scholars of the 1930s gave much time to preparation for class, but not much thought to it.

In the mutual attempt of educators and subject-field professors to ignore each other, the believers in subject won hands down. In most universities that had grown from colleges, if not in all state universities, schools of education went their own way, free of concern from the arts and sciences. Parents could understand and appraise the methods of schools of education without help or interference from the specialists, and they could disapprove of specialists for being specialists; as parents, they were aware of no aid from the masters of specialized research.

A few professors of literature wrote intelligibly on literary subjects for middlebrow quarterlies, monthlies, and weeklies; what these amiable scholars wrote for learned journals was generally intelligible but of no general interest. That they scrupulously employed footnotes has brought Anthony Grafton to their defense two generations later and has seemed sufficiently illustrative of academic quaintness to bring wide syndication for a *New York Times* piece citing voices today against Grafton's argument that footnotes lend moral authority. "Academic journals," says the *Times* author, "are still a stronghold for scholars who use footnotes to demonstrate their accountability and their sources (or flaunt their erudition)."[5]

Most scholars, with liberal views they thought it safer not to express publicly, out of lethargy ceased to address unprofessional readers. Yale's William Lyon Phelps made the circuit of ladies' clubs as though he were Emily Post, but his equitable treatment of *Twelfth Night* and pie-in-the-face farce did not encourage colleagues to seek that kind of otherwise welcome supplement to meager pay. Most thought it more dignified to drive a taxi at night, which some of them did.

After catching up with Galsworthy, Lawrence, and Conrad, and getting through a public library copy of *Anthony Adverse*, they read poems and essays by Eliot and poems by Yeats; truant reading included Hemingway, Fitzgerald, and perhaps Stein, Aldous Huxley, Evelyn Waugh, Rose Macaulay, and Rebecca West; most were beginning to read Auden and Woolf. They held in high respect translations of Proust, Kafka, Mann, and Malraux. The magazine *Story* taught advanced students and faculty new literary uses of the vernacular. For a minority, the restless desire to teach poets later than the Edwardians and Georgians brought Robert Frost, Hilda Doolittle, Vachel Lindsay, and Carl Sandburg into anthologies for the classroom. If photocopying had existed instead of the ditto and mimeograph machines that dirtied the hands of departmental secretaries, modernization of the canon might have grabbed the coattails of the little magazines—which were about to become, chiefly, organs of criticism.

Almost all teachers of poetry published later than 1789 were aware that I. A. Richards in *Practical Criticism* (1929) and F. R. Leavis in *New Bearings in English Poetry* (1932) had gone beyond Eliot in challenging their literary values and educational methods. Discontent with context was as inevitable as defection from philological precision had been. This was no longer a world in which writers addressed the "gentle reader."

CHAPTER THREE

The Growth of Care in Method

Among the many ways World War II served as water-
shed, the double reverses in higher education deserve
more than a footnote in the social history of North
America. From factors not yet fully determined, but
certainly among them the Great Depression of the
1930s, the percentages and numbers of women earning graduate and professional degrees, which had
risen after World War I, had declined by 1940. When
young men left ordinary life for military camps,
Europe, and the Pacific, class lists in graduate schools
shrank to near nothing. Professorial eyes looked
through tears at empty chairs even in respective
offices where they had enjoyed individual conferences.
For exercise, they spurned colleagues German in origin and sympathy.

The yearning by faculty for students was more
than satisfied when the Servicemen's Readjustment Act
of 1944 (the GI Bill), with its subsidies of living costs as
well as tuition, brought a crush of returning soldiers,
sailors, and fliers into higher education in 1946 and
after. Women among the GIs were as ready as the men
for further education, and the return of men in
1945–46 to interrupted lives nudged other young
women out of wartime jobs and into college. Neil L.
Rudenstine's short history of efforts at Harvard to
achieve geographical, religious, economic, occupation-

al, ethnic, and sexual heterogeneity includes no other shove toward diversity of students equal to the GI Bill.[1]

The war had taught congressmen the need for precise knowledge on many subjects that had been previously thought to deserve little more than idle curiosity. That the Soviet Union had emerged as a major, apparently uncontrollable power loomed above all other reasons for promoting pure and impure research. Colleges and universities utilized the GI Bill to expand both research and teaching. Community colleges required more and more Quonset huts, before acquiring brick and stone edifices. With the acquiescence of Congress, universities not otherwise able to meet the costs of expanded enrollments inflated their accounts for educating veterans. In one common procedure, they charged the national government with full tuition for veterans writing dissertations by creating courses on paper only (when other doctoral candidates at that stage were charged a small fraction of full tuition); in another, state universities charged tuition for in-state veterans equal to that for out-of-state students. Mandated expansion could not have occurred without the GI Bill and probably would have suffered early curtailment without the Cold War threat of nuclear destruction; from obligation and the need of minds trained for quantum leaps in technology, research for the defense, health, and well-being of the nation began to concentrate in graduate and professional academia.

The President and Congress agreed in 1945 on a "coherent, statute-based policy to aid knowledge-creation in the nation's universities," a policy that required formation of the National Science Foundation in 1950.[2] The flow of money into universities made possible a reduction in classroom hours in order to promote research. Research in universities expanded for the same reason it continued at Raytheon—the nation's fear of nuclear extinction. Einstein wondered why professors, presumably not below average in intelligence, continued to live and work in New York City. Because of nuclear capability, departments even of literature could compete for larger numbers of faculty, somewhat as vice presidents compete for numbers of employees to gain relative power within the bureaucracy. In the competition for holders of the Ph.D., "assistant professor" replaced "instructor" as the rank and salary for the first three years out of graduate school.

The Ford Foundation employed generous funds and various devices to urge legislatures, educational organizations, and smaller foundations to work for increases in the numbers and sizes of educational institutions. It pleased parents and officials in small cities that with financial support from state and nation their two-year institutions could expand into baccalaureate colleges; in middle-sized cities, the local college could now, with impunity, advance a step or two steps upward with master's or doctoral degrees. The University of the State of New York had been "a supervisory (not a teaching) body exercising a general control over all the [private] schools of higher instruction." Like New York, Massachusetts and other states expanded state-operated systems of higher education from near zero to networks of colleges and universities vying in complexity with what the railways had been and the hub system of airlines would become. The holder of a Ph.D. in English who had been teaching freshman composition had no time to lament the explosion of numbers while blissfully designing one or more courses in the specialized field of the previously closeted dissertation.

In the nationwide expansion, Ohio University in Athens and Ohio State in Columbus spread their branches. But when with more evident drama Kent State, Cleveland State, and Bowling Green State expanded tenfold almost instantly, the explosion required a simultaneous multiplication of teachers at Kent, Cleveland, and Bowling Green for classes in freshman composition. The obvious solution required the inauguration in those proud places of doctoral degrees in English, in order to offer teaching assistantships successfully to holders of master's degrees from elsewhere.

Accrediting agencies and the well-meaning officers of the Ford Foundation made the mistake of believing that the nation needed vast new numbers of PhDs when the evident need was vast new numbers of dedicated college teachers, with or without the doctoral degree. Besides offering fellowships for doctoral candidates who seemed likely to earn the degree in less than four years, the Ford Foundation prodded learned societies into recommending reductions in a range of requirements for the degree—fewer fields of study, fewer languages, less draconian standards. As early as 1962 the Dissertation Committee in English, appointed by the Ford-funded Woodrow Wilson National Fellowship Foundation, protested ineffectively, as the president of Williams College did, that the capable, full-time college teachers needed to meet the increased enrollments did not all need to possess the doctorate. Complaining because the qualities of dissertations of great promise as well as requirements were being reduced to award rapid completion, I resigned from the committee for 1955–56—but compromised that stand for teaching by going abroad under a research fellowship.

The numbers of PhDs increased almost exponentially. Circumstances conspired to reduce the Master of Arts degree to insignificance in institutions converting GIs into PhDs. Insistence on the highest research degree for college teachers in the humanities has brought in later decades neuralgic pain to every part, from head to unemployed fingers and toes.

With the numbers of both undergraduate and graduate students suddenly enhanced, the Ph.D. remained a research degree, but strains in departments of the humanities mounted. College teaching was not Mark Hopkins on one end of the bench and a single innocent child on the other. Young veterans of foreign wars sat in large restless classes next to students a few years younger but media-informed if not streetwise. All were likely to ask, among other Why's and Why Not's, how the novice teacher could show them the significance of Tennyson or Plato for their movie-smart lives. In graduate study, where the morbid anxieties were not sexual, professors had not prepared young teachers of *The Mill on the Floss* who had been away several years for questions about contraception—but they also hadn't prepared them for any other question undergraduates were likely to ask. Graduate professors had tried by example as researchers to convey total divestment of personal interest.

Returning soldiers, sailors, and fliers failed to comprehend students five or ten years younger who seemed to feel themselves unique victims of nuclear threat. And, since Nisei students submitted stories or essays about detention as children, didn't the boys who thought "the War" occurred in Korea fail to write poems or even "themes" about it because nothing of interest had happened? Before the generation gap became news, Hitler had created it; in higher education, training for research enforced it.

Professors who had long enjoyed superiority over educators who supervised practice teaching suffered greatly from the thought of turning the Ph.D. into a degree for college teachers. Candidates received from the lowly head of the composition staff, however, direction and advice they could use immediately in their first full-time position, which would increase their skills at correcting weekly themes—students write? they can't even type.

PhDs who had pursued literary study and completed a literary dissertation without serving as teaching assistants in composition had no preparation for teaching logic and rhetoric, clarity and force, to freshman. Those who had earned tuition as teaching assistants felt that they had already spent too many evening and night hours correcting spelling and punctuation. Even those who had primarily sought training in research, rather than a license to teach in college, looked upon the next step, an instructorship under misers who hoarded all the courses in literature, as a soul-deadening apprenticeship. Why could they not teach what their graduate teachers taught? They dedicated hours, energy, and thought to the chore of correcting compositions but experienced little of the potential joy of realizing that their correction of weekly essays improved the quality of citizenship in the nation, while their graduate professors continued to meet halfway their responsibility to prepare teachers of British or American literature to teach teachers of British or American literature.

New instructors luckily elevated to the teaching of what they had studied entered a world of dramatic change at the teacher's desk or lectern. Undergraduate teachers new and old talked in the classroom directly about the poem or short story or novel currently open on every desk in the room. Seeds for this change had been nurtured in the 1930s and had sprouted as seedlings in the general absence of students in the early 1940s. Its American beginnings can be identified in the influence on T. S. Eliot of Irving Babbitt, New Humanist author of *The New Lao-coön* (1910) and *Rousseau and Romanticism* (1919), the T. E. Hulme of posthumous *Speculations* (1924), and other anti-Romantics discoverable to Eliot in France. Ironic modernist poetry seemed to demand a new criticism, not contextual and not straying into anecdote. The New Critics charged that the scholars had practiced journalistic gossip; certainly the scholars had not often strayed from context into analysis or analytic judgments.

The New Critics were conjoined with other "new critics." In *Practical Criticism: A Study of Literary Judgment* (1929) I. A. Richards demonstrated that Cambridge University students read and judged poems with spectacular incompetence. Also at Cambridge, after Richards moved to Harvard, F. R. Leavis as lecturer, in his quarterly *Scrutiny*, and several books, notably *New Bearings in English Poetry* (1932) and *The Great Tradition* (1948), narrowed the canon by attacks on Spenser, Milton, Shelley, Fielding, Thackeray, Hardy, and others. William Empson, a student at Cambridge under Richards, continued brilliantly the New Critical attention to paradox and ambiguity. These and other new critics thought it charitable to say that literary historians, like their musicological cousins, had the misfortune of being deaf to tone. In the view of innovators, both the linguistic- and the historic-minded scholars were like the cellist always expressionless because he detested music. The new critics set out to restore attention to language, not as history or in general but as the printed content of a single, autonomous literary artifact. The new criticism emphasized diction, syntax, and form rather than inspirationally motivated content; its foreshadowing of Marshall

McLuhan's proclamation, "the medium is the message," neutralized the political inclinations of the professoriat. At Vanderbilt University, John Crowe Ransom gathered among his Southern Agrarians Allen Tate and Robert Penn Warren. Denis Donoghue, in "The Practice of Reading," cites and quotes Leavis, Richards, Ransom, Wilson Knight, and others to show how they returned the focus of literary study to language and how they differed from later critics influenced by social studies.[3] Ransom moved to Kenyon. When the *Southern Review*, with Warren as one of the editors, published essays by Ransom, Tate, and Kenneth Burke but displeased the governor of Louisiana, Huey Long, Warren completed the line of New Critics "gone North," extending from Yale to Michigan. Despite the inclusion of Warren, it was predictable that the southern conservatives would find the political and social interests of most humanists to have taken a reprehensible direction.

In a major proclamation, *The New Criticism* (1941), Ransom consolidated his earlier emphases on criticism as professional knowledge of literary techniques, professional but to be promulgated among young writers of poetry and fiction. Warren and Cleanth Brooks edited a textbook, *Understanding Poetry* (1938), that brought both a narrowed canon and specific exegeses into classrooms from 1945 through the 1950s, with diminishing use thereafter. A sequel, *Understanding Fiction* (1943), extended the new critical influence on teaching methods but could not be employed, in class and out, in the same monolithic way as a selection of lyric poems with rules for explication of each lyric. The new criticism was not an escape from linguistic emphasis but a return from attention to context for a new way to emphasize language. R. P. Blackmur and Donald Davie, among other critics of the period, came to the brink of saying what became a commonplace later, that the individual author is a recording device through which language speaks.[4] The New Critics ended for literary study, except in encyclopedic handbooks, belief that paraphrase can convey the "meaning" of a poem.

Every teacher knows that a student given the choice between a traditional and therefore conventional course and a new course will choose the one never given before. For young teachers of English, the new criticism entered with an appeal stronger and deeper than its novelty. Most had chosen doctoral work in the field of English from a love of reading literature. Here was an opportunity, not to apply one's training but to practice what one had thought to be the learned profession chosen, to teach literature, verbal beauty. Few GIs who carried a B.A. degree into graduate study in the humanities realized that they had stepped into a career of research as if accidentally into a pile of manure. Now, as instructors encouraged to publish in learned journals, they could prepare for class by close reading, discover a previously undeclared ambiguity in a stanza by Keats or Dylan Thomas, and publish the discovery in the *Explicator*. Close reading by the whole species in undergraduate classrooms brought commonality of method to teaching but not to research and publication.

Many old-timers who now explicated the open text as they stood before undergraduates and by the late 1950s sat in seminars explicating with graduate students, did not, apparently, know why they did it. They continued research as literary historians with little change beyond apology for exercising the intentional fallacy. Besides objecting to what they regarded as undue attention to intellectual control, exactitude, ambiguity, and paradox, they took delight in refuting ingenious explications by New Critics who assigned to a word in a poem of the seventeenth century meanings that the *Oxford English Dictionary* seemed to prove unknown before the twentieth century. For the stubborn, relativity had not proved the twentieth century conflated in time with the seventeenth.

Uneasy at confronting the possibility of a road less traveled by, they congratulated each other on discovering upstart critics in acts of devotional expatiation, blind not only to anachronism but frequently to typographical error; Fredson Bowers caught two prominent critics in extended ecstasy over Yeats's Aristotle as a soldier, exegeses based on a New York printer's metathesis from Yeats's "Solider Aristotle." Scholars complained that any edition, however flawed, could now serve the critic's purpose of exercising personal ingenuity on a text. The time had not yet arrived when a critic would respond that "Solider" could allow and encompass (not mean) "Soldier." Punctilious scholars accepted unhappily Eric Partridge's demonstration that "die" in poems by Donne and other Metaphysicals carried the doubled meaning of sexual orgasm. It had not been their habit to discourse on a *double entendre* of that sort.

The argument of critics that students of literature had not for the previous quarter of a century had a subject they could call their own, a subject free of biography, history, and social context, appealed to younger teachers. The appeal of such critics as Blackmur, Empson, and Kenneth Burke to a select audience aspiring to intellectuality, lent repute to lesser, imitative critics more readily understood. The psychological, social, and political observations of Lionel Trilling and the nonacademic (and antiacademic) Edmund Wilson created a bridge by which reviewers in the monthlies and weeklies could cross toward more reclusive critics. Over such bridges instructors in English did as much to expand the readership for *Ulysses* as the prolonged notoriety that Joyce's novel shared with D. H. Lawrence's stylistically accessible *Lady Chatterley's Lover*. For the public that subscribed to book clubs or frequented the neighborhood bookstore, however, professional literary study seemed more and more to employ the linguistic devices of *Finnegans Wake*. What had happened to college as they had known it?

Before 1940 a professor could lecture on Monday and Wednesday on the social and political surround of the work or works being read, dominant genres and changes in genre during the period, influential precedents for the work in hand, and minor authors in the surround. On Wednesday he or the rare she could present biographical details, summarize proclamations on literary subjects by the author or the "school," and list in chronological order on the blackboard other works by the author, whether Dryden, Congreve, Fielding, or Carlyle. The blackboard—how else could information be propagated?

On Friday the professor could, and the conscientious did, distribute blue books and write on the blackboard questions to be answered: "How far are descriptive passages in this work successful in serving what you take to be the central theme?" "How successful is the handling of point of view in this work?" "What characters serve as foils to each other? How might the contrasts have been improved?" The blue book came back to the student with a grade and informed rebuttal, not later than Wednesday to be effective and usually on Monday. The professor as lecturer stuck to surround, the student read the next work with the remarks on last week's bluebook in mind. In this way the educational procedure of the 1930s, designed to be informative, could challenge the critically uninstructed student to read subsequently assigned works with attention to technique. No student after 1945 could have such joy of reading with an innocent eye. Intellectual independence thereafter could have only the pleasure of debate with discourse external to the assigned text.

I. A. Richards had demonstrated clearly enough that stress on literary history left the average undergraduate unable to find in poetry much more than vague emotions. For the college student already an experienced reader and sensitive to language or literary values, however, freedom to discover previously unperceived values and to express personally formulated opinions improved on the foundation of adolescent pleasure in undirected reading. Such freedom to discover became paradoxically reduced by the arrival of close reading. While theorists became increasingly insistent that neither critic nor author could identify intention and no single meaning of a work or a word was determinably probable, undergraduates were increasingly deprived of freedom to interpret. From Maine to California, nearly every student enrolled in a survey of English literature now took notes on some version of the same explication: The speaker of Donne's Holy Sonnet 14, with violence tempered by form, began by asking the three-personed God to beat on him like a tinker mending a pot, like a wrestler throwing his opponent, like a blacksmith utilizing hammer, anvil, bellows, fire—all three assaults paradoxically that he might be restored upright and whole, and all three because he now needed divorce from God's enemy, the Devil, in a usurped town (his body).

It is hardly debatable that Sonnet 14 includes those examples of paradox and that few undergraduates could have found them without help. Students who would have been incompetent readers under the old dispensation became under the new *informed* readers. Half of the students returned some portion of the explication on the final examination: Donne battered three persons who besieged his hometown—a wrestler, a tinkerer, and a blacksmith. Richards was proved more than right: most students couldn't read poems, and they couldn't listen either. Students equipped to be engineers echoed the explication accurately but could not identify the paradoxes in the next sonnet assigned. Students destined for graduate study in English returned the exegesis improved by other interpretations that diligent search had uncovered. Later, as graduate students, they would be asked to employ greater independence in exercising approved methods of close reading. The most successful would explicate in a dissertation a body of work by a single author, find a publisher for the dissertation, and teach the dissertation to undergraduates.

After 1945 prominent critics of the new persuasion could safely leave to disciples propagation of method at annual meetings of the Modern Language Association and other conferences. For several years explication and the job market at the annual MLA meeting created such eagerness that only hotels in New York and Chicago could accommodate the up to ten thousand who attended. James W. Tuttleton of New York University remembers a stage when teachers reluctant to abandon scholarship adapted the newer methods of explication:

> Taking literature more or less on its own terms, the teacher saw his task as being that of the advocate or expositor of theme and form, representing in some sympathetic way the aims, intentions, and achievements of the writer. Some mix of history, literary history, and biography, brought to bear on a close reading, provided a general method of understanding the text and the context.[5]

Bringing knowledge to bear on a close reading afforded a silken transition from information purportedly disinterested to unconscious prescription for what to think.

A third factor joined World War II and the new criticism to transform the teaching of literature in colleges. The transformation into close reading could not have occurred without the sudden availability of paperback books. The method of teaching by explication in the classroom could not have swept literary study so completely after World War II had not this congenial revolution in publishing made its material and substantial contribution. In Britain, just before and during the War, Penguin Books had begun to issue literary classics, in paper bindings of different colors to distinguish genres one from another, and Penguin rapidly published more titles, and more copies of each title, than the venerable and more expensive clothbound Everyman's Library and Oxford World's Classics. First among books inexpensively studiable in America came the waddling entrance of Penguins.

Before the war, classes in literature had been taught primarily from anthologies. Even in French courses, where nearly all works available to students were paperbound, the expense of individual works had made anthologies dominant. For classes in English literature and the courses in American literature steadily expanding in number, anthologies had included lyrics or other short works and passages from longer works by authors regarded as major, with brief selections from a sizable number of minor writers. These proportions held both for general anthologies used in introductory surveys and for anthologies confined to periods— Medieval, Renaissance, eighteenth century, Romantic, Victorian, Edwardian-Georgian. Lecturers had little reason or none to require that these heavy anthologies be carried to class.

Distribution of the Modern Library, the most popular series of reputable books in the United States, had been directed toward the general reader and not the classroom. With class use shown by Penguin to be a possibility, Bennett Cerf began to invite academic scholars and critics to provide informative introductions, although the words of each classic continued to be assembled in the way customary among such series—the pages of two copies from an older cheap series were mounted on larger sheets, spelling and capitalization were altered in the margins, and new galleys were rapidly proofread. If the word *not* were omitted or inserted in *Gulliver's Travels* by a printer not up to Swift's irony, the printer's error remained.

Several publishers became sensitive to the demand for texts that could be open on every desk in a classroom and sensitive to the inroads quickly accomplished by Penguin paperbacks. The Riverside series of Houghton Mifflin, with Gordon N. Ray as general editor, and the readier, more inexpensive series from Henry Holt began to replace the large anthologies of earlier decades. Cheap books served close reading of a narrowed canon. Croft's Classics, pollarded almost to a stump, could be supplemented by the Signets and NALs produced for a wider audience, on paper so acidic it began to crumble at the first touch but with luck would survive for a school year—with the student's classroom notes no more illegible at exam time than they were when entered on the narrowest of margins. The cheapness of Signets and NALs encouraged teachers to add the spice of fiction contemporary with the nominal poetry of the course—an early trend toward an eventual retreat from close reading in the classroom.

The low price of paperbacks made possible an alertness to changing tastes. In the Depression era bulky anthologies were sold from one class to the next, year after year. Professors throughout the humanities had hesitated to change anthologies lest students avoid the course from lack of cash for a new book. *English Poetry and Prose of the Romantic Movement*, edited by G. B. Woods, continued virtually unchanged from 1916 to 1950. The 1950 edition introduced eight pages of "Romanticism in Illustration," with enlarged attention to one of the "forerunners," William Blake: a typically fruitless attempt to meet the new competition. Palgrave celebrated in his *Golden Treasury* "Scott, Wordsworth, Campbell, Keats, and Shelley"; close reading and paperbacks locked the cellar door against two of those previously treasured poets.

The availability of paperbacks made possible nationally an increase of courses devoted to long fiction. Residual effects of philology had left the study of fiction less respectable than study of poetry or drama, but a major deterrent before the avalanche of paperbacks was cost. For instructors stooping to fiction, an anthology had covered the early years by including *The Castle of Otranto* and selections from Richardson's *Clarissa*. Now even students without the support of the GI Bill could afford copies of ten or a dozen novels from *Robinson Crusoe* or *Pamela* to *Lord Jim*, or in translation from *Don Quixote* to Gide's *Strait Is the Gate*. Lyrics could be photocopied, novels not.

With the great increase in number of students, competing anthologies for each literary period typically ranged from slightly revised editions of the one previously dominant, with selections from lesser writers and works illustrating the surround, to one making space for middle-length poems by covering only authors thought quintessential, with reduced annotation that left the teacher free to explicate. The venerable, conventional anthology of seventeenth-century poetry could now be supplemented economically with separate paperbound selections from Milton, Dryden, and some third favorite of the teacher's. Close reading and inexpensive editions reduced the canon progressively. Now the student in Romantic poetry, a field restored to prominence by M. H. Abrams, W. Jackson Bate, and Harold Bloom particularly, could afford separate volumes of selections from Byron, Shelley, Keats, Wordsworth, and Coleridge (including some prose) and could afford in the narrow margins to make notes on the teacher's explications. *Don Juan* and *The Prelude* (1850), like *Paradise Lost*, could be bought and studied in editions light enough to be carried about with ease. Producing affordable Blake took a little longer. Lesser writers, failing to qualify for analysis of texture, soon disappeared as if into Bunyan's gulf that hath no bottom. The Matchless Orinda and Felicia Hemans faded along with Abraham Cowley and Barry Cornwall.

Besides changing what had been a field without boundaries, where there was no authoritative list or canon, the new methods made close reading what Ransom had called for, a professional action, a licensed procedure. When one professional now asked another, "Have you read *The Wings of the Dove*?" the answer from one who had read Empson's *Seven Types of Ambiguity* had to anticipate combat, "Well, I've read it, but I haven't really read it, you know." A colleague in political science or sociology who remarked, Martini or dry Manhattan in hand, "I got a charge out of reading *Bleak House* last month," met a chilled sigh or a catechism on why F. R. Leavis recommended ignorance of any Dickens longer than *Hard Times* or, more amiably, the promise of a list of keen readings of *Bleak House*, which would show that only professionals knew how to *read*.

Polite custodians of literary study would not at that moment have commented on how right Mencken had been about the booboisie, but any answer they made would have been one more step into isolation from the general public. Retreat into isolation had perhaps been predictable from the turn of the century. Modernism created a chicken-or-egg enigma: had a bourgeois, capitalistic society evicted its artists, or had superiority of vision enabled aesthetic royalists to slam the door against society? Why had the Modernismo of Spanish America found echo in poets who could not have been influenced by it? Had the slogan of "make it new" been simply the way chosen by outcasts among other possible ways of living in exile? Leading authors and painters made being pariahs seem congenial.

British authors born after 1870, in the last three decades of the reign of the Widow of Windsor, applied the epithet "Victorian" to moral and aesthetic principles they chose to repudiate. While scores of Edwardians and Georgians were achieving the popularity they sought, a few, initially self-selected, could see that the realms opened by Flaubert, Verlaine, and Cézanne allowed no place in the junta for Somerset Maugham.

After Conrad and James complicated narration in novels of the early 1900s, Virginia Woolf advanced from acceptance of fiction as mirror in *The Voyage Out* (1915) to the fluidity of consciousnesses in *The Waves* (1931). Joyce traveled from the symbolic nuances of the realistic

Dubliners (1914), through the autobiographic myth and curbed irony of *A Portrait of the Artist as a Young Man* (1916) and an anthology of prose styles for the transformation of myth, syntax, consciousness, and id in *Ulysses* (1922), onward to the contrived obscurity of cuisinarted language and convoluted allusion in *Finnegans Wake*, published in 1939. Although academic humanists were not initially responsible for the widening gap between highbrow and middlebrow, even professors not prepared to teach Modernist writers could share their sense of distance from persons too wholesome to read Gide or Joyce.

Approval of T. S. Eliot's ascendancy and Picasso's financial success could heighten the sense of superiority over materialistic acquirers. If you admired Pound's cantos or Barnes's *Nightwood*, why attempt to address bankers or cereal-packagers? Poets found in language no opportunity for exact equivalents of visual abstraction as it descended from Kandinsky; the action painting of Arshile Gorky and Jackson Pollock did not lead directly to improvisation in performance by poets; but poets could retreat from emphasis on meaning and could share with Surrealist painters instinctual and Freudian approaches to dream with results unexpected by serene readers of Kipling and Noyes. As fascination with the Freudian unconscious invaded most humanistic fields (up to the edge of academic psychology), it need not be counted among the vagaries of literary study that excluded the general public. Nor was the reach of Sartre and Camus evident only in the academy: weeklies became aware that you get no soul from God or society; if you want one, you must make it. In that era a Unitarian who believed in character rather than in Atonement could run for the presidency, although unsuccessfully, against a general. Professors of literature, not at the bottom of the scale in ill repute, but ignored, attributed evident neglect to their share in the mutual contempt of intellect and corporate business, putting them, they hoped, in a league with Joyce, Schoenberg, Ussachevsky, and Rothko.

During the peak years of Modernism few current writings by philosophers had been taught as literature, but a common past made fluid the boundaries of literary and philosophic study of the "old sages." After 1945 analytic philosophy became the dominant and then the exclusive study in departments of philosophy. Specialists in linguistics found in analytic philosophy a kindred subject, but students of literature felt as excluded as the general public from procedures beginning in the assumption that only what is necessary to science exists and demanding such apparent periphrases as "is it the case that there can exist an *x* such that." It seemed an alien case of knowing how to do things with words. Yet teachers of English and French could only envy the claims of scientific exactitude in the questioning of whether meaning could be assigned to words through the intention of a speaker, and indeed whether "words could have determinate reference at all."[6] Holders of the Ph.D. in philosophy who continue to believe in common language and the old sages can now teach ethics in schools of business, law, or engineering, just as historians can find in their students of business or engineering believers in the possibility of knowing facts about the past. Despite the contraction in philosophic method, the occasional influence of analytic philosophy on the way scientists have conceived their purposes, methods, and conclusions points to a world outside the prison of literary study.

Doubtless the replacement of eclectic procedures in literary study by defined limits and attempted precision was driven chiefly by the prestige and rewards afforded the alarmingly more exact sciences. Suffering a progressive increase in inferiority, as one scholar left in the rear of "deadly scholasticism" puts it, "the humanistic disciplines needed to set out to discover, or 'manufacture,' high-octane subject matter . . . to evince proof of possessing esoteric knowledge that a mere reading of books would never confer."[7]

With change in the arts and the humanities continuing through the 1950s, Congress and governmental agencies in Washington divided their own and everybody else's anxieties between secret military research and fear that the Soviets were stealing our secrets. With the launching of Sputnik, the first artificial satellite, in 1957, the Russians demonstrated decisively that they had stolen a secret we didn't have. Humiliation increased in 1958 when Charles de Gaulle attracted worldwide attention by calling the much smaller first satellite of the U.S., Explorer I, *un pamplemousse*, a grapefruit not of Californian size. Congress answered at once with the National Defense Educational Act (NDEA), for the encouragement of science, mathematics, Russian, and other modern foreign languages.

Physicists, acknowledging their value-free responsibility for atomic and hydrogen bombs, thereby endangering humanity, sought ways of atonement. Mistrusting the claims of social studies to scientific precision, physical scientists urged support of the supposedly value-filled humanities. Physicists in guilt over the nuclear threat to humanity offered to share funds in the hope that academic humanists could restore human values and faith in virtue. The cloak of NDEA graduate fellowships soon extended to comparative literature, history, philosophy, English as a second language, and finally on to American and English literature.

The appeal from scientists exposed for the first time publicly the actual situation: humanists no longer believed themselves custodians of value. Very few citizens in North America had less faith in the power of great literature to improve moral character and emotional stamina than the teachers of literature in higher education. When a Senate committee gave leaders of the constituent organizations in the American Council of Learned Societies a week's hearing to help Congress spread the largesse of NDEA into further disciplines, each answer was a variant of "Senator, I can't explain to you what we do." Hubert Humphrey summarized for his fellow senators what the delegates had not, could not, or would not say: English professors and their graduate assistants teach the leaders of the decades ahead to think and communicate clearly, to form and express thought in a fusion of logic and feeling, and from a better comprehension of great works of literature both to understand and control their own conduct better and to sympathize more fully with the variety of their fellows in the human family.[8]

Ransom's noble intentions for literary study incorporated claims similar to those generously bestowed by Senator Humphrey, but *Scrutiny* and the *Kenyon Review* changed the content of academic articles without closing the divide between intellect (Empson) and morality (Leavis). Leavis and Ransom provided new patterns for imitation. With the rise of creative criticism, originality in research and discovery completed a transition already begun into reversal and refutation. Articles continued to begin with the citation of books or earlier articles to be refuted or qualified in the following pages, but citation was a habit rather than any longer significant. Citation continued to give the editor of the journal publishing the article some confidence in its originality.

It is rare for a humanist to plagiarize consciously and rarer for humanists to falsify data or findings in the way pressures occasionally drive scientists and medical researchers to dissemble. In the humanities the pressure to publish produces more often facsimile and mediocrity. Imitative mediocrity in published explication had the one advantage for classroom teaching that it dealt directly with works of literature, with some chance that it dealt with works the students were asked to read by teachers who had read explications intelligibly repetitive in method.

René Wellek's and Austin Warren's *Theory of Literature* (1942) served largely to warn against language that might suggest acceptance of exploded historicism rather than serving as applicable theory, but doctoral candidates began to write dissertations applying the methods of a particular critic to selected works of a single author. Northrop Frye's *Anatomy of Criticism* (1957) provided one applicable method, especially for pigeonhole categorization within genres. In 1961 Wayne Booth would provide in *The Rhetoric of Fiction* (revised in 1983) intelligible terms for what would become "narratology." Dissertations utilizing Arthur O. Lovejoy's identification of "ideas" as peripatetic kernels of thought, the structural anthropology of Lévi-Strauss, the archetypal grids of Karl Jung and Maud Bodkin, or the Neo-Aristotelian compromises of Ronald Crane were soon outnumbered by dissertations utilizing reader-response theories from Wolfgang Iser, Harold Bloom's pain and spur of belatedness, John Searle's speech-act theory, Gérard Genette versus mimesis, Tzvetan Todorov's narratology, the new mythologies of Roland Barthes, or Jacques Lacan's emphasis on language in psychotherapy.

The representation of three or four of these approaches in a range of books by academic authors on George Eliot or Conrad, but not of all these approaches, left the way open for further books on Conrad and Eliot. The first paragraph would provide a justification: "There have indeed been several fine books recently on Conrad, but nobody has yet shown how Lacan's theories can be applied to illuminate *Nostromo*." A candidate committed to Iser's reception theory but dissatisfied with a book applying it could offer a dissertation refuting the book or refining its argument. With prices increasing, such books would be purchased by university libraries and by most doctoral candidates planning to dissect the same author in a dissertation, but could be afforded by few others. By the 1970s several prominent university presses announced that they could no longer invite the submission of any work devoted to a single author. Bad books did not as such drive out the good, but together they destroyed the market.

Whether or not college teachers of literature noticed how quickly such books were left at the gate in the race for novelty, they now felt a more urgent need to purchase books on literary theory. An essay by Michael Riffaterre, influential in marking the transition from explications commending structural unity to a level of severer discipline, demonstrated the inappropriateness of analysis less stringent than the most precise among readers' perceptions.[9] Critics at Yale, more boldly than others, proclaimed the independence, artistry, and ascendancy of critics, in language more academic than that of Oscar Wilde in "The Critic as Artist," which anticipated their claim: "I would say that the highest Criticism, being the purest form of personal impression, is in its way more creative than creation, as it has least reference to any standard external to itself, and is, in fact, its own reason for existing, and, as the Greeks would put it, in itself, and to itself, an end." Accepting the

Arnoldian proclamation of ascendancy, critics of intellectual austerity began designating their work as a kind of literature, to replace the no longer admired easy-chair essays of Hazlitt or Gosse. Samuel Johnson could no longer be evoked, because he had crowned his old age with *The LIVES of the English Poets.*

The term *imaginative prose* used in the present study to distinguish the deliberately fictional from *expository prose* was abandoned by more precise critics for the generically precise *discourse.* The search for precision of vocabulary, based on subtle distinctions and even more on avoidance of looser traditional terms, led to an accumulation of innovative terminology from each discovered critical voice, with a result far from precise: not dear reader, but implied reader, intended reader, authorial audience—these variants even in suspect arguments where "the author" is regarded as relevant. Terminology that detractors call jargon is original and incisive only once; it becomes self-apparent by imitative repetition and dilution among apostles of the original user but remains jargon to others. Not every theorist is a jargonist, and much theory has deserved freedom from esoteric vocabularies.[10] Terminology-clogged books have been enlivened by spurts of wit, and splendidly useful critical studies have sprung ideologically from a base in rigid theory, but an intelligent public that found the literary scholars unutterably dull now can protest additionally—and they can quote—the comically unintelligible.

Literary theory as a branch of philosophy and a kind of literature can justify high claims for itself. As philosophy it has exposed careless vocabularies and sloppy thought. As a kind of literature it has pumped energy into teachers of English and French. Unless, however, the teacher can explain why certain literary works have merit superior to the teacher's as critic of those works, why maintain the academic scaffolding of literary study to support the critic's claim to an independent discipline? If the irrefutability of a particular critical approach comes to be granted, is society advanced by its demonstration in each of the chronological periods departmentally maintained? May it not be wondered if theory is one more way to avoid the general significance of literature?—*je déteste la musique.* What is a businessman or molecular biologist (now become university president or dean) to say when asked by a legislative committee why the state should pay English teachers? What is the poor fellow to say they do other than argue with each other about how literature should be read and taught?

In *The Great Tradition* F. R. Leavis identified superior works while assuring the young that life does not afford enough time to read such novelists as Fielding, Thackeray, and Dickens; he knew because he had read them. With a little ingenuity replacing Leavis's moral fervor, his method could dispose equally of the novelists he rescued, and indeed it has been so employed. "Forget D. H. Lawrence; I have been made to read him, and I know."

Since some time before 1970 few English professors have had time to read Fielding, because reading time not given to authors in their specialty has gone into reading critical and theoretical debates, apparently in a wan hope that some view will ultimately prove decisive. Kenneth Tynan, unmoved by an objection to his inaccuracies in commenting on a play newly opened in the West End of London, answered that the job of a theater critic was not to be accurate but to serve the stage by attracting attention to it. If inadequate on truth-telling, Tynan was right about service. Whatever the method of study, only literature already written can give importance to those who profess the field as theirs. Yet to say that literature is in custody would currently delight the purported custodians by its ambiguity.

Thomas S. Kuhn's *The Structure of Scientific Revolutions* (1963), arguing that each generation of scientists has followed a different paradigm, lent a strong impetus to the general relativism. It shook philosophy into supplementing attention to scientific method with attention to the history of science; for literary critics it measurably decreased their sense of inferiority to microbiologists. Relativistic revision had broken the horizon to signal a new day. No one in academe predicted accurately what the new day would be like.

CHAPTER FOUR

Disruption, Deconstruction, and Diaspora

The ascent of theory increased the confidence with which professional students of literature looked down on the chasm that separated them from the common . . . no longer *reader*, perhaps, but common eye for images, common consumer of icons. But more momentous changes, events larger than literary study, offered confidence no support. Among the less serious changes, a progressively smaller proportion of the brightest men were entering graduate study in the humanities. The ratio of women to men in the humanities improved steadily. Most graduate professors were men, but women had become the majority at the top of nearly every class. Threats to patriarchy and its chauvinism were beginning to be explicit.

Campuses had ceased, as if suddenly, to be places of isolation from life. That the system of military conscription exempted a sizable proportion of college students from experience in Korea or Vietnam made many of them uneasy and restive. On the campuses of large public universities as well as in private institutions providing refuge for the privileged in the new sense of deferment from service, opposition to the war in Vietnam came in part from divided conscience. The religious questions, "bewilderments, frustrations, disillusionments, and egotisms" noted by Northrop Frye[1] made sophomores at the University of Wisconsin, typically, appeal to a lecturer on Milton for further guidance on religion. Protests in the South and in Third World countries became imitable events. A sizable number of students from colleges outside of Dixie had seen action in the march on Washington in 1963 if not earlier in the growth of the civil rights movement in Alabama. The Student Nonviolent Coordinating Committee was enticingly named.

Students weary of deferred gratification discovered kinship with Allen Ginsberg, William Burroughs, and other protesting Beats, and made a bible of Herbert Marcuse's *One Dimensional Man* (1964), which described the repressions of industrial society, and the desire of the United States to exploit the Third World and dominate the earth, as *sexually based*.[2] Catherine Gallagher's history of literary criticism pertinently notices that "the absence of the category of pleasure in most critical studies" made Ransom and Brooks less appealing guides than Susan Sontag to students of the 1960s.[3]

When university police at Berkeley tried to arrest students promoting the Congress of Racial Equality in 1965, Mario Savio, returned from Mississippi to Berkeley, saw that the university administration would strengthen, by its opposition, a Free Speech Movement. At Berkeley and elsewhere tensions between administrations and students rose steadily between 1965 and the dramatic events of interest a few years later to all public media, when marches, demonstrations, padlocking, occupation of university buildings, and sporadic violence spread from campus to campus. Administrators, mayors, police, and editorialists opposed the protests with means not always superior to student ingenuity. Sympathetic views of the protests by reporters, recorded on front pages of the *New York Times*, contrasted with opposition in the editorial pages.

The planned overthrow of the old regime in the Modern Language Association employed successfully tactics that on individual campuses brought temporary or lasting chaos. Democratic, Marxist, feminist, and other previously impeded aspirations, including a prolonged adolescence in some, came together with spontaneity when awakened in individuals.

On Morningside Heights in the spring of 1968 the gradual increase of decibels in drumming, voices, and miscellaneous noise throughout an afternoon announced the approach of a bold action. In Cambridge later, ominous silence into and beyond sunset preceded the smashing of windows in Harvard Square. Common to the extremes of noise and quiet, paper of every size proclaiming adamant opinion was thrust into hands, faces, and trash barrels. As in the Paris of 1789 paper fell like snow. Students of mob violence had an expanding laboratory for research.

Most faculty members in the humanities and social studies sympathized sufficiently with the protestors' cause to lean toward justification of the means. Professors and graduate students collaborated in effective education free of the institutional superstructure. The superiority of conspiratorial education to institutional requirements, examination, and grading was a genuine lesson, even if soon forgotten. However conspiratorial, most professors felt morally compromised by the success of the Students for a Democratic Society's leaders, who proclaimed and practiced disruption but gained what they simultaneously sought for themselves as individuals: out-of-classroom education and academic degrees to be conferred officially by harassed presidents. Few of those leaders anticipated that students who distrusted or detested them would share the gains in freedom and power.

Roger Rosenblatt's *Coming Apart* reminded Mark Helprin of the Harvard faculty's "moral collapse in slow motion" and betrayal of "the ideals of liberal democracy" by its failure to insist on permanent expulsion of radical leaders.[4] However it may have been at Harvard, most humanists, who had chosen a lifetime of education over combat, salesmanship, or management, were reluctant to take the side of their employers and the police against any who had been students in good standing. Few who had survived wounds in Europe or the Pacific would have entered the humanities if they had previously made a completely free choice of patriotic heroism. To promote faculties into the cause for the death of academic liberalism circa 1970 is strong hindsight but partial history. Somewhere near the mean among professors of literature a peripatetic, liberal, uncertain individual leans upon a firmer system of liberal tradition for support. It can be more accurately said that fence-sitting by humanists, whether from individual character or a blending with peers, contributed its bit to the death of academic liberalism ca. 1970.

Nor did professors of literature adequately realize that the objects of student complaint included the direction, the *aims*, of graduate education. Charles Moore, the dean whose students of architecture at Yale became leaders in student revolt, recognized that students objected in part to the "prescribed direction" of study, and acknowledged that schools "cannot persist in training people for a vanishing role."[5] In architecture the prescribed direction meant Beaux Arts or its ouster by minimal Bauhaus formalism; in literary study it meant compartmentalized history or its opposite in any antihistorical approach espoused by a given teacher; to students generally it meant regimented progression, tests, and ranking.

With discord mounting, university presidents could look forward to an average of three years in that peculiarly embattled position. Presidents who had risen through each rank of the faculty felt the comedy of regarding the relationship as a natural enmity. With direction uncertain, academic bureaucracies increased in power and continued to expand. It was in the 1960s that university presidents and their development officers, grappling with the present, lost all vision of the institutional future. "Presidencies" would become management. If faculties envisioning a collegiate future succumb to further attrition, managers will construct a postsecondary education deprived of its past.

The events of 1968–72 drove a wedge into individual minds and split previously tolerant faculties into radical and conservative minorities and a paralyzed middle. The temporizing described in Rosenblatt's book about Harvard occurred in every large university. Faculties in that crisis were symbolically representative of a national population that watches two obstreperous parties obstruct government in Washington.

With the failure of national purpose in the decade before 1973, hope for a Rousseauistic General Will, "when the voice of duty replaces physical impulse and right replaces appetite," became a farcically remote ideal. Liberalism withered or, in some, was simply passed on the way from radical revolt to a correspondingly extreme reaction. I can give small witness, though, that the besieging chaos, sewing seeds of new diversity, brought unwonted cooperative unity to the department of English and comparative literature at Columbia University in the early 1970s, very much as a sense of external threat induces coalescence in a nation. Severe external threat in the 1990s, less physical, has not been perceived within the humanities as an adequate reason to unite. Teachers in departments of literature have not asked what of significance they have in common besides sanctuary in the same department.

With student demonstrations not ended, an analysis went out from Michigan to warn other university presidents that disruption seemed to begin with tutelage from teaching assistants in English and sociology. As investigation revealed also that everywhere the larger department, English, had envious rivals, administrations could encourage faculty proposals and faculty votes on carefully considered ways to reduce the number of graduate students in English then teaching sections of freshman composition. The course could be reduced from two semesters to one, and it could be taught by graduate students and assistant professors or seniors from all departments interested enough to feel qualified for the task of teaching freshmen to write. As one alternative, the course could be abolished and each teacher of an introductory course using natural language could require prose compositions and correct them for clarity and vigor. Another alternative, still in force in the University of California and elsewhere, would allow all applicants for undergraduate study to place out of "Subject A" altogether by passing, before entering college, one test or another thought to demonstrate competence in writing. All of the alternatives for reducing contact between teaching assistants and freshmen—reduction or elimination of freshman composition, distributing responsibilities among several departments, avoidance of the course through adequacy in SAT scoring or administrable tests in writing—all served to reduce the cost as well as the numbers of teaching assistants in English but increased the instructional cost to the institution for the course load of each freshman.

One or another of these defensive actions occurred in a number of universities, but nearly all of those that reduced the required course in composition to one semester or quarter later reverted to a year of it, and most that temporarily enlarged the pool of instructors later decided to bestow again upon teaching assistants in English the activity of marking twenty to ninety essays a week. The threat of revolution fomented by graduate assistants waned, but the threat prodded a few smaller and middle-sized universities to institute, in addition to logic and rhetoric, first-year seminars taught by senior professors from most or all departments. Thus one large hill formed after a volcanic eruption brought forth something better than a molehill.

The recurrent disruptions of academic slumber in 1968–72 will not be forgotten by any who acted or witnessed, whether in anxiety or in elation, but the business of learning resumed repeatedly between disruptions. The 1960s seemed to many in the 1980s to have left little trace, *Fussstapfen,* if any, not of Bigfoot but of a Shelleyan angel touching the mind like the memory of a dream. The sudden shrinkage of new positions with and without tenure in 1971 came with a heavier tread. The Ford Foundation had successfully promoted an increase in PhDs; only the Mellon Foundation seriously attempted in the 1970s to rescue for higher education the best minds that faced everywhere the same announcement: "Closed."

In the 1970s many professors and students of literature who acted in diverse political causes and environmental movements adopted and held theories that denied any direct relation between literature and the world of action and actuality. Some caught in this paradox wondered if they had chosen the wrong vocation; others disregarded the contradiction in the assurance that literary study needed radical reform whatever its theories. Meanwhile, theory spread like molasses. There seemed to be a thirst, as if from previous drought, for "elaborate technologies of reading."[6]

In the 1970s English departments suddenly competing for the few identifiable African-Americans who had overcome the system began also to discuss timidly the propriety of following French departments in the appointment of a theorist, or maybe compromising on a specialist in the history of criticism. The least painful solution for most large departments was to appoint a recent PhD of their own who had shown an aptitude for theory. Like elevating a young person into courses on film to join a historian of language or an analytic bibliographer as oddities, appointing a single theorist added further to the problems of planning the future of the department, for tenure continued otherwise to be awarded to those fitted for openings by period of specialization, medieval to contemporary. Ah, dear mother of God, wasn't it worry enough that they had no specialist in Irish drama?

Over against the search of anthropologists for the distinctively human—reason, speech, tool-using, the opposable thumb, abstraction and symbolism, a sense of comedy—theories in the search for critical finality sought freedom from humanistic assumptions. Undergraduate teachers dubious about theorizing nonetheless feared that avoidance of the subject in the classroom might send their students toward graduate study in literature with a fatal deprivation.

Almost all new ideas entering departments of literature in the seventies found a funnel through France, although some had originated within the Soviet Union or earlier in Russia. Julia Kristeva discovered that Russian critics before and after the Revolution had emphasized dialogic statement and counterstatement in all speech in a way to foreshadow her own severer intertextuality, the production of new discourse by earlier utterances. The decline of German had not entirely prevented American interest in the economics-minded Frankfort School, but it helped strengthen the influence of French literature and critical theory. With Sartre, Beauvoir, Artaud, and Céline subverting moral conservation, Jacques Derrida crossed the Atlantic as littérateur credited as philosopher and joined Michel Foucault, credited as historian, in declaring the insignificance of authors in the transmission of language, a claim, as Mark Twain said of reports of his death, that exaggerates both the nullity of authorship and the scope of literary influence. As Ferry and Renaut argue in *La Pensée 68*, Derrida, Foucault, Althusser, and Lacan exaggerate equally the philosophic weaknesses of humanism.7

To reject, for example, analysis of the relations between the poems and the surviving letters and reported remarks of Johnson, Gray, Keats, Tennyson, or Eliot is to suffer sheer loss of knowledge in order to sustain a theory. Mark Twain and Samuel Clemens are not identical, nor are S.T.C. and Coleridge or H.D. and Hilda Doolittle, but these pairs have a genetic relation that cannot be imposed equally on Saki and Shenstone.

In the professional journals, under the sway of theory, much thought went into style, into witty ways of employing jargon, but the effect of choosing one of three or four prevailing theories to apply was often to make all works of a given kind prove the same point. From an opening paragraph, and sometimes from a punning title, the rest could be predicted. The theory chosen determined within a narrow range the argument to be made. Theorists taught one way of reading all works of a genre, or at most two or three ways, not sensitively intelligent response to the individualizing characteristics of differing works. Even new roads were cluttered with terms more predictable than intelligible. The chief disadvantage of perceived novelty in any field is that the incompetent and the lazy believe and try to practice it. In the heyday of theory, imitation practiced second-degree jargon.

Scholarship on Elizabethan drama, combining printing history with textual logic, demonstrated thoroughly the value of physical evidence for interpretation and therefore for the principles of interpretation, hermeneutics. For another example, over against the accumulation of physical and textual evidence by collaborative Blake scholars, most independent theory after the 1950s looks like cumulative self-deception. Explorations of illuminated printing by Robert Essick, Joseph Viscomi, and G. E. Bentley Jr., conjoined with scores of others studying meticulously Blake's fusion of invention and execution, have transformed understandings of Blake's accomplishment. I do not say that we have made these discoveries available for their widest potential audience, but they are of greater import for the study of Blake than any disembodied theory has been. Almost every interpreter of Blake has added something in the dialectic advance of comprehension, Hegelian proposal, counterproposal, and synthesis. Much of this accomplishment has been aided by the increases in stringency of literary theory. The complexities of Blake's own dialogic texts have made his work an awkward subject for deconstruction and for revisionary historicism; but Robert Ryan, in *The Romantic Reformation* (1997), can first clarify the complexities of text and then appeal to historical context, not to clarify further but to increase the persuasiveness of his clarifications. His insistence on the orthodoxy of Blake's belief in the Son of God who became flesh for humanity rises from a firm base built through an incremental increase in knowledge by earlier scholars.

The deconstructive mode introduced by Derrida, intensified by Paul de Man, practiced and persistently defended by J. Hillis Miller and others, displaced Romantic organic unity and the New Critical unity of metaphorical contrivance (the procedures that introduced Formalism to America) with theories of the indeterminacy and self-contradiction in all language. Building on Ferdinand de Saussure's demonstration that the link between what is signified and language as signifier is always arbitrary (the word *woman* is not feminine; if *meow* seems more feline than *bow wow*, linguistic chance has made it so), Derrida and other deconstructionists declared the signified, erroneously called actuality, to be equally arbitrary and uncertain when we reach for it in speech. If any word signifies one thing it also signifies the opposite. What the language of a poem seems to reveal as present contains the opposite by its absence—both presence and absence remaining indeterminate. Deconstruction declares the complementarity of the unknowable. Whatever is present in discourse was "always already" representationally present before language gave the text on the page its parlous being.

Deconstruction begins in a willful exaggeration of the difficulties of communicating thoughts and feelings in a natural (Wittgensteinian "ordinary") language. *Paideía*, education, for Derrida always corrupts to *paidiá*, play, linguistic pastime. If Bacon on truth would be too harsh—"What is truth? said jesting Pilate; and would not stay for an answer"—then in keeping with Kant's description of the aesthetic as disinterested free play of taste, Derrida has practiced a variety of playful literature rather than a branch of thought. The claims to have eliminated humanism were contradicted, were always already refuted, when the proclaimers joined humanistic literature by attaching their names to individualizing claims of originality. Denis Donoghue's approval equally of Arnold, Pater, and Wilde's advice "to see the object as in itself it really is not"—an approval of Barthes, Derrida, and Pierre Macherey for a lack of interest in "the works under consideration"—is an approval of exciting examples of literature, not of methods of literary study.[8]

The oddity is that disciples of Derrida and this aspect of Nietzsche proceeded as if Kant in concluding that God's existence cannot be proved by reason had proved that no god can exist. Unable to know the past, they chose to act as if it were never there. When Derrida says, Not I, he does not therewith speak for disciples.

Richard Rorty has welcomed Derrida as a colleague among "philosophers who deny that there is any such thing as the correspondence of a belief to a reality," philosophers who believe that no reality outside of mind can be known; but less subtle minds in literary and cultural studies have not been able, like Rorty, to use the old language of truth as a human convenience or to argue that "honesty, care, truthfulness, and other moral and social virtues" remain unaffected by relativistic freedom of mind from reality.[9] Some literary deconstructionists have been unable to look on history as a convenience in Rorty's way rather than in Michel

Foucault's. The issue is the degree of autonomy assigned to theory; Darwin, the most patient practitioner of the empirical method known, had to have a theory, but he did not let the theory determine the course or the result of inquiry.

In an era of suspicion and jaundiced journalism, we have chosen models for a culture of suspicion. Michel Foucault, who remade the past in his image, cannot be denied a kind of earnestness, but almost every generalization made by Foucault can be refuted by the disinterested attention to data thought honorable by literary scholars of the 1930s. An exception may be his belief that knowledge is control, that rationality inhumanly suppresses those that reason arbitrarily declares insane.

In theory "death of the author" and death of actuality have conjoined. True, Adolf Schicklgruber did not personally do all the things historians say "Hitler did . . ." and revisions in history will ensue without end, but there is a great distance between those recognitions and declaring the Holocaust or the Reign(s) of Terror in France a representation that cannot be represented in a different way from fiction. *The Great War and Modern Memory*, by Paul Fussell, as itself representation shows most significantly that representation is typically a part, but not all, of what history signifies. We can say only of fiction that judgment of it should not depend on belief or disbelief that its events have occurred. The proposition that nothing can be certain should not incorporate a unique certainty for this proposition. To paraphrase James Kastely on Aristotle's inventive rhetoric, literary study, after determining the roots of indeterminacy, needs to offer an earned and relatively stable closure.[10] Knowledge enables wiser action. We can never achieve certainty, but we can learn and distinguish enough to improve action.

Critics remaining inside the cage describe such language as that in these paragraphs as obtuse, which may not misrepresent the quality of mind responsible for these pages. The tone here probably comes most of all from a sense that esoteric subtlety is not our greatest need just now. As an aspect less serious than loss of internal commonalty, but serious enough, professors of literature are hired hands that need like animals in a zoo to be fed. Toward literary study regarded as logic-chopping in opaque language, some are antagonistic; many more are indifferent. Within departments of literature, postmodernism has not made professors confront the world we continue to live in; planes fly, computers calculate, managers plot, half the populace reads—but what?

Retreat into theory, though, is not mutiny within the fortress; it is one more impelled decision to defend a very narrow defenseless pass. A yearning for precision has brought humanists into a confined area of uncertainty. In the world outside, fortunately for society, distrust of knowledge has not replaced evidence as a value in courts of legal justice.

I stand with those who regard most of the victories of theory after 1950 as unfortunate for literary study and its place in communicative society, yet to wish it away, to wish nothing new and different to happen, would be to stand tall with the Newhouse News columnist, James Lileks, who proposed on July 21, 1997, that the National Endowment for the Arts be retained with enough funds for a community theater to put on *Show Boat* but not enough to encourage the production of innovative art.[11] Custodians of literature need at the very least to avoid feeling bogged in inaction, and illusioned ingenuity is perhaps better than repetitive pedantry, but inaction, pedantry, and closet ingenuity are equally irresponsible. "Make it new" is an inadequate aim. From theorists we have come to perceive much more about authorship, from theory we have begun to practice new distinctions, but we have found only each other as willing depositories for what we have learned. Focus on theory has intensified an unearned vanity. Good work has been done, but it is as if we accomplished the basic research for which no application was ever to be sought, nothing that served any purpose beyond the sharpening of minds—like the sharpening of knives for display under glass in a museum. A profession shrinking and in retreat is not helped by leaders who enjoy the illusion of winning.

That self-enclosure has added strength to enemies of the academy should be of far less concern in the humanities than the crippling of its own recent graduates. A victim of the system describes one practical consequence:

> I hope the liberal arts can become less hermetic and self-contained, so future humanists will not go through my difficulties if academia shuts them out. I hope their programs will provide them with options and strategies for alternative employment. It angers me occasionally to think such realistic guidance was not part of the humanistic culture I came through.[12]

Graduates regarding themselves as unemployable except in the fields of their training have suffered doubly because managers, legislators, and the public have seen no reason to maintain the numbers of full-time teachers in a field grown hermetic.

Some of the narrowing came from a yearning for precision. Exactness could not be claimed without precise terminology, which in the event encouraged a lot of esoteric obfuscation. Contrast with the language of professionalized theory the introductory words of Pickering and Hoeper's *Literature*, an anthology for the needy: "Contrary to rumor, literary criticism is not always an exercise in human ingenuity that professors of English engage in for its own sake. . . . Literary criticism is nothing more or less than an attempt to clarify, explain, and evaluate our experience with a given literary work." [13] The editors of that volume go on to recommend learning as much as we can to appreciate fully "a truly great work." Skepticism, deserving respect for its utility as a brake on pride and enthusiasm, loses its vocation when the engine of pride loses power. To seek power currently within literary study is to seek power in a flower bed with a fence around it. The writers called men of letters, however contentious among themselves, seemed as a class companionable spirits pleased to communicate genially with an unrestricted audience, and thus *served* literature. Transmission of what Matthew Arnold called the best that has been thought and said does not require pride even in human accomplishment if the transmitting carries delight and self-awareness to each generation.

Poetry, drama, and explorative fiction propagated by colleges have pleased, informed, and enlightened persons who were to achieve positions of leadership or who then occupied such positions, and many of these leaders have believed serious literature helped them to understand better both themselves and others near and distant, helped them to refine conduct, helped them to rejoice in the good, helped them to bear sorrow, suffering, and defeat. It remains true, and I repeat, almost the only persons in North America hesitant to make such claims for literature are those who, paid to teach literature and regarding themselves as crudely underestimated by the society around them, enjoy the intellectual strength of preparing others to teach greater precision and caution in reading to still others who will propagate these skills among the wounded, the self-chosen. Outside, a soil not barren asks for fertile seeds.

H. W. Fowler's *Modern English Usage*, under *humour*, described irony as seeking exclusiveness by addressing an inner circle in a way to mystify others. I would not have the scores of brilliant theorists and brilliantly ironic new historicists reduced to my so-so level, but if modesty and a sense of prostitution are required for address to a wider audience, the situation calls for modesty and prostitution. Journalists who sample sessions at the annual meetings of the Modern Language Association hoping to find a comprehensible reassessment of a major author have settled instead for stories with such headlines as "Professor Says It Ain't Wrong to Say Ain't."

Much in literary study need not be readdressed to a wide public, but what can be readdressed should be. The burden of restoring communication rests with the academy. With most scholars and critics addressing each other, outreach has come largely through chance and intermediaries. A large body of common readers was intrigued to learn through unacademic reviewers of the "anxiety of influence" and the death of intention. Readers and legislators and voters should know the best and the worst from academic scholars' and critics' own word processors. Readers satisfied with the earliest editions of the Modern Library, made (as already mentioned) by mounting for the printer pages of earlier unreliable series, will not know what has been replaced by the principle that no definitive edition of an author is ever possible, but the clearest practicable exposition of such principles should be available to most who read and to all who buy books.

It is a partial good that college-trained novelists and poets can be supported economically as teachers in a nation where legislative bodies have no high regard for reflective minds (including legislative colleagues who reflect), but restriction to academic experience is a kind of contraception against creation of the Great American Novel. Literature does not gain new strength when novels from the cloistered fortress can be praised for being, not perceptive about academic life, which would be claustrophilic enough, but significant primarily for sophistication of device. Even the oversea Nabokov's novels from Ithaca, *Pnin* on the way to Pynchon, bear the mothball aroma of the academic closet. Professors teaching academic fiction have more reason than most for relaxing with narratives of detection or fantasy.

Much in the aspiring science of narratology, such as distinctions among story, narrative, and plot, and among narrator, implied narrator, the old "point of view," defined reader and implied reader, it makes sense to know. If Balzac and Thackeray were only half conscious of such distinctions, and James's prefaces and notebooks oblique and imprecise as guides, fiction has nonetheless practiced the subtleties of narratology since Job and Genesis. The distinctions of metaphor, synecdoche, and metonymy that faded with the fading of rhetoric revived usefully within literary study in consequence of Roman Jakobson's association of metonymy with contiguity and realism in contrast with metaphor, based on similarity with difference, as the main trope of symbolic artistry. But academically trained fiction, introducing further subtleties of technique to be admired as variations on narrative, threatens to merit William James's assessment of his brother as being able to do everything to a story except tell it. The academy, which has produced both author and audience for such fiction, would do better to teach undergraduates exactly, *exactly* what is wrong with novels by John Grisham and Danielle Steele.

We academics need to say in a letter to the world what we can show in the classroom, that reading profound literature is fun, that unlike addictive narcotics it can both brighten and deepen the reader's ordinary life day-to-day. We need to discover, describe, and propagate current fiction that affords deep and lasting pleasure. That such intensely superior fun rests on epistemological uncertainty should be a minor issue in a society losing touch with the printed page. Outside the college teacher lies a reachable world. It is a greater value for future legislators, employers, and patrons to know what literature can do than to know how it does it.

The science of narratology tends to give the surgeon increasing self-satisfaction from progressively intensified dissection. Virginia Woolf's suggestion of a second reading for review after a first reading for pleasure surpasses the idea of *really reading* as the only way to enter a book. Although to an analytic mind two variously inadequate readings do not end in adequacy, Woolf's suggestion aided more than one generation on repeated journeys through *Middlemarch* and *Lord Jim*, and helped a smaller number through *Nostromo* and *Daniel Deronda*.

Feminism, the activity that began to be organized within the academy on behalf of women's rights and concerns on approximately the date Betty Friedan founded the National Organization for Women (1966, NOW), promised literary study a way out of self-enclosure. To whatever degree language spoke through women, what they said in protest against patriarchy pointed toward what common speech calls actuality. Outside the academy lived women, and men, receptive to protest against palpable inequities, persons capable of distinguishing between virtual reality and either potholes in the street or exercise of authority. Adrienne Rich, able to learn from Simone de Beauvoir and other feminists how to enlarge a poet's audience, began to say both "read me" and "we can overcome." The MLA was by 1968 female in sufficient numbers to make it a promising and appropriate place at first for combat and then for justified domination.

How far, it had to be asked, should the reality of gender interfere in the contests of theory? Freud had to be refuted along lines leading to Julia Kristeva and Hélène Cixous. Renewed attention to Freud uncovered landmines that diverted attention from actuality. *Die Traumdeutung* of 1900 had initiated the extremely usable conviction that the writings of an author, already shown by Freud to be unaware of unconscious motivation, held such latency that the absent was always present. Freud's prescription for interpreting dreams, fearlessly exposing dishonesty at the core of human consciousness and precise in its definitions, can be exercised with rules like those of "The Modern Hiawatha"—"Put the inside skin side outside." Unobstructed pursuit of motivation is less like legal justice than like professional ice hockey; there are rules but few prohibitions. Such pursuit can release all restraint in an intellectual's search for power. The professor of English or French as literary theorist addresses others in the fortress, the equivalent of seeking power in a kindergarten, but the professor as biographer can gratify an audience almost as large as that of a journalist exposing a politician's corrupt search for power almost from infancy. (In a maneuver to lessen exposure of my own aggressive motivation, the examples that follow are less than current and utilize intermediate objectors.)

Passages in Lawrence Thompson's massive biography of Robert Frost were paraphrased by a biographer who had earlier declared literary history a passé genre:

> The reason to write poems or to graduate first in your class (as Frost did) is in truth to get back at your enemies by surpassing them or wiping them out. The reason to want to excel at being a pitcher is that it provides you with a "lethal weapon" to throw

at somebody's head, perhaps permanently dispatching him. What look on the surface to be benign, time-honored ways for a young man to distinguish himself—in scholarship, in aesthetic creativity, in athletics—turn out under the Thompson microscope to be in fact ways of "retaliation"—ways expressed by the biographer in melodramatic terms.[14]

Phrases from a life of Jane Austen have been similarly cited: Austen's remarks on one acquaintance "reek of pettiness"; on the death of another, she displays "cold-blooded nastiness"; with regard to her brother James, Austen is "astonishingly bad-tempered," with "open resentment" revealing "more than mere neurasthenia." *Northanger Abbey* is "the work of a caustic, disappointed woman" who snarls in a "paroxysm of rage"; in *Pride and Prejudice* there are "strains of cynicism and nastiness"; *Sense and Sensibility* is "bleak and black and nasty" throughout; in *Persuasion* Austen's "fangs show through in undisguised harshness." "Could she have been . . . jealous and resentful of the happiness she was forced to provide" for her characters?[15]

Depreciative biographies gain reviews in weeklies having wide readership as most adjustments to critical theory do not. A biographer can thus share power over an author with readers who were bored by assigned novels as undergraduates and who would be unable to hear Austen's ironic voice in the gracious films of the 1990s from her narratives. Authors of books claiming intellectual and moral superiority over a writer or other accomplished figure as subject seldom apply a Freudian scalpel to their own motivation. Often, consciously or unconsciously, they have simply hitched a ride on fame and accomplishment.

Such biographies have been one way to reach publishers, reviewers, and a wider audience. If negative biographies sell more copies than judicious biographies, can teachers in the humanities be proud of acquiescing? If confession of sin no longer sells as well as speculative revelation about one's famous parents, is it our vocation to approve the low road? Of Andrew Delbanco's *Required Reading: Why Our American*

Classics Matter Now (1997) reviewers who have taken English courses in any college can now ask: Doesn't he elevate the authors of these American classics into too much nobility, into a category of human conduct excessively moral? Isn't it a critic's responsibility to find cracks? Wasn't Melville deep down a congenital liar? How could he not have been? We have become close students of what Cotton Mather called sin. The first of Ricardo Quintana's books on Swift, *The Mind and Art of Jonathan Swift* (1936), made news in its day by revealing a sane Swift that only the innocent had previously embraced and the suspicious in a later era would be embarrassed to find or to search for.

Denuding biographers and some deconstructive decoders of a text (for a smaller audience) compete with the opera directors, unable to look down far enough to find Mozart's or Verdi's librettists, who have Violetta sing "È strano! è strano!" lying where she has been directed to fall, under a bed or otherwise justifying the belief of American audiences that she is crying "I am strangled! I am strangled!" It need not be so. On film and video with lipsynching, vocal power need not be directorially diminished. Franco Zeffirelli's *Otello* film, utilizing his excesses on stage, heightened Verdi as Verdi's librettist Boito tightened Shakespeare—with advances in each mode of representation. A distinction can be readily made between a different perspective offered to the prevailing cultural climate and Nietzschean license to shock or to pamper present sensibilities. Robert Wilson's genius is not to decorate a work incongruously but to overlay it disinterestedly with vital, independent images; deconstructionists at their very best perform a similar feat. But the very best is rare in any game. Designers for opera and drama of panoply have so far not specialized in virtual costumes, to exploit the nakedness of Noah their father. The postmodern, poststructural specialty is virtual allegory.[16] Much psycholiterary theory, when applied to particular works, has practiced similarly oversimplifying ingenuity. Like denigrative biography, these are ways to claim authority for appropriated merit.

Although conservatives have made the language of deconstruction sound repellent to ears as far away as the today-show, talk-show public, its methods have spread successfully from departments of literature to other disciplines. Deconstruction drew the interest of historians through a Foucauldian attention to history in departments of literature. The New Historicism, as instituted and named in Renaissance studies by Stephen Greenblatt at Berkeley, provided a political approach to complement the aesthetic that descended from the New Critics into such well-knit studies as Helen Vendler's of Keats's odes and Shakespeare's sonnets. New Historicism compromised by making use of such immaterial Marxist theorists as Walter Benjamin, Theodor Adorno, and Louis Althusser and by proceeding similarly on a road where philosophic disciples of Marx (who had been among the earliest to make a structural realignment of history) encountered Nietzsche.[17]

The New Historians went beyond the scholars who first objected to the arbitrarily unifying procedures of such books as *The Elizabethan World Picture* by E. M. W. Tillyard but thought descriptions of unity a good teaching tool. Jerome McGann could owe to Arthur O. Lovejoy's *Essays in the History of Ideas* (1948) the argument that "Romanticism" has always borne contradictory meanings, but the New Historians have been productively successful in calling attention to ignored tensions and hidden codes within what Lovejoy had designated "ideas," and McGann, conscious of inevitable current bias, denies in several seminal studies that the inheritors of romantic ideology could evaluate Romanticism without distortion. Examples of self-delusion were required to demonstrate the value of the insight, but theory should not obscure the possibility that some authors and artists have been capable of describing honestly and with more than average accuracy what they were up to.

Like other recent theorists, New Historians have fed into excellent studies attention to the broad implications of detail. If Marxian historicists often invent tenuous and dubious filaments between fashions of behavior and the implied or absent in literary works, as literary historians they get closer to life as we experience it than conventional emphasis on scheduled public events; by advancing current social causes more openly than the literary scholars of the thirties whom they in several ways replicate, they have succeeded in awakening some of their readers to the life of others around them. Marxists would not get so abstract in theory that a narrow canon of elitist literature could keep them from turning toward popular entertainments, folk arts, movies, television, newer forms of interactive visual culture, and the relation of these media to the impoverished and underprivileged. Their dedicated studies of Marvell or Browning or Eliot are excellent for those suffering from the same wound, but these remain as tedious as the next academic literary study to the non-Marxist and the unwounded, to those who are uninformed concerning literary criticism either by choice or by exclusion.

Offspring of the marriage of Marxist and deconstructionist theories, the new literary historians have tended to construct analogies between shapes or movements in vocabulary, syntax, or tropes in the literary language at hand and shapes or movements in the economic (capitalist) surround. Traditional scholars protest that it is difficult enough to identify convincingly the shape or movement of an imaginative piece of literature without superimposing undemonstrable generalizations imported from systems external to the work. But in truth, certainly in what is currently construed as truth, that which is superimposed can have no secure foundation beneath it. Devotion to complementarity and indeterminacy has successfully overthrown for our time, and not merely by excesses, humanistic claims for knowledge over information. What for our time is left, information—lists of books, of cities, of buildings, of words (without definitions), a record of the baptism of a poet's only known daughter dated in the parish register April 10, 1694—has served, for example, in refuting (to the satisfaction of fellow scholars) a speculation based on lack of information. Beyond bald data, however, almost everything in literary study, including the Marxian elements, derives from preconception. Professors of literature can now begin with the song quoted by H. G. Wells, "I don't 'ardly know where I are," and end with John Gay, "I thought so once, but now I know it," meaning I completely don't know how to tell where I are. If Allan Bloom's title and argument in *The Closing of the American Mind* (1986) violate the canons of tolerance, he is surely right that the replacement of belief in truth with all-encompassing relativity comes to education with a high cost.

Women's studies, the New Historians, and ethnic interests required what the deconstructionists had not practiced, a realignment of the canon. New reading lists led to new anthologies that include materials previously neglected, particularly writings by and about women and documents from intellectual and social contexts of "belles lettres." Anthologies that would have been too burdensome physically in the decades of word-by-word examination of paperbacks in the classroom are again viable when general issues supplant attention to linguistic detail.

The success of the New Criticism and competing theories in giving students of literature a sense of having a room of their own, exclusively theirs, has also invoked a challenge to departmental integrity from interdisciplinary cultural studies. As Gerald Graff and Michael Warner argue, the dramatic rise of theory, making clearer what had been taken for granted before, opened for debate the subjects of purpose and method in literary study.[18] The debate has widened. Professionalization of critical language was a prolonged experiment that failed sufficiently to encourage the exit of ethnic studies from departments of literature.

Ethnic study, a countervailing force to austerity of language that germinated in 1960s theory, impinges directly on departments of literature by socializing their subject. In so far as cultural studies begin in reaction against arid theory, they are a malady seeking health. As a social force, they meet a perceived need and an evident propensity. Although much recent theory makes no distinction between fiction and what has been thought not to be fiction, theory concentrated on belles lettres until the multicultural revived arguments about content. Thus far, in looking outward from ego and self, the multicultural parallels the revival of figural art.

Within global commerce, industry, communications, and politics, cultural studies offer relief from academic Eurocentrism. The multicultural lays a restraining finger on the greatest scourge in Euro-America, the claims, traditions, and institutions of racial superiority. It has brought, as Lawrence W. Levine says in *The Opening of the American Mind*, "a more eclectic, open, culturally diverse, and relevant curriculum" (171). As a development in higher education, however, the multicultural also advances perceptibly the disease of complexity. Multiculturalism is not responsible for turning uni-versities into multi-versities; it may, however, help them become mille-versities.

Literature approved by the elite had already been conspiring to encourage ethnic studies by drawing upon intellectual sources parallel to those of French theory. The turn from character to structure in fiction found one master in Italo Calvino, but poetry and fiction the most impressive in all the world had suddenly enjoyed a diaspora from Hispanic America. Professors of drama in the 1930s could declare with impunity that all the plays of Lope de Vega put on one tray of a balance would not outweigh in value the weakest play by Shakespeare. Dante and Goethe stood tall in major literatures, Cervantes was thought to tower alone. Even in 1953 a distinguished Spanish scholar found "a relative absence of real novelists from the Spanish-American scene" (and from Brazil); nor did he admire the poets.[19] But suddenly no critic, however scholarly, could ignore the Latin American masters in a half-century of imagination, intense observation, and bold sex—fluent Mistral, surreal Neruda, Paz, Carpentier, transcendently skeptical, cryptographic Borges, Andrade, Allende, Fuentes, Vargas Llosa, Lispector, fantastically real Donoso, and others, perhaps above all pityingly detailed García Márquez, in his own metaphor giving ink the ambience of blood. Offering unfamiliar life reshaped in language, rather than language manipulating situation as in late Joyce and middle Nabokov, these Latin American writers provided sufficient stimulation to impel Hispanic studies. As one consequence, academic humanists have been asked to choose between intensive study of uncoupled cultures and world literature, mostly in translation. Powerful literatures, past and current, exist outside our continental borders to be found and employed for the enlargement of character, intellect, and sensibility.

There are complaints in foreign language departments that literature courses for upperclassmen, emphasizing multicultural contexts of literature, are neglecting or altogether abandoning language.[20] Multicultural and multimedia approaches within departments of language and literature have a less clear rationale than similar approaches in interdisciplinary programs.

The impulsion to be postmodern in the world of Humpty Dumpty after the fall has not distracted the nation from the business of sports and other realities of television. When demands in the 1960s for African-American studies grew into the multicultural, however, alumni and alumnae with tears for Mr. Chipps learned from Hilton Kramer or the Kristols that the old school had gone to pot in their absence. The titles of a hundred books, not only by attackers but by insiders promising a few corrections, tell the story, not as fiercely as some of the subtitles, but clearly enough: *Higher Education under Fire*, *Crisis in the Academy*, *The Imperiled Academy*, *Education without Impact*, *Killing the Spirit*, *The Closing of the American Mind*, *Illiberal Education*, *Coming Apart*, *Escape from the Ivory Tower*, *Profscam*, *The Hollow Men*, *Coughing in Ink*, *Tenured Radicals*, *The Abandoned Generation*.[21] Humanists felt a degree of flattery in being treated as significant by the Regnery Press. Teachers of literature, accustomed to neglect as harmless drudges or undecipherable sophists had begun to draw attention as incendiaries betraying the citadel.[22]

Enemies have had no trouble detecting change. The annual directory of members, institutions, and departments in *PMLA* lists separately more than six hundred women's studies programs and more than one hundred and fifty institutions with ethnic studies, with as many as six programs in a single university. Study of the problems, contributions, and opportunities of women has been biased enough to call forth Robert Bly for manhood but presumably can be exonerated from the charge of being local. It is not a virtue that ethnic programs meet local needs more often than they offer an academic currency nationwide, but voiced approval is by no means local. Among papers of the Nineteenth Symposium in English and American Literature at Tuscaloosa published in 1996, all but Stanley Fish welcomed the breaking down of barriers that would have preserved tradition. Gerald Graff, here as elsewhere, called for coherence without disciplinarity.[23]

Ethnic and gender studies attempt to integrate distinct approaches and disciplines. Integrated liberal studies in which all subjects correlate have attracted bright students who emerge more richly informed than those who have majored or concentrated on a single subject. Until recently, administrators and conservative critics have concurred in proposing such integration of disciplines as a way of saving students from the suffocating isolation of departments. Presidents can be expected to encourage covertly this sterling opportunity to reduce departmental power over curricula and appointments.[24] Even a bitter enemy can distinguish between "a leftist political ideology that sees all cultures, their mores and institutions, as essentially equal," and multicultural education, that "presents and examines the values and practices of other cultures objectively and critically."[25] The distinction should be clear to administrations even with the omission of "leftist." Relatively objective programs could provide models, needed throughout higher education, for service through interaction with "the community."

Graduates from an integrated ethnic program can be conversant, if intellectual hurdles are kept high, with a greater range of disciplines than those whose focus has been a single traditional department. If programs designed to raise political consciousness survive that purpose, the hurdles can be raised. Meanwhile, the political aims of key multiculturists will enable them to rejoice in any dissipation of established power and established entities. This is not at all to say that political bias has no proper role in ethnic studies. Socioeconomic research in a center for Mexican American studies can provide, for example, a salubrious counterpart to analysis by management of the methods and conditions in the maquilas, assembly-line factories of the border. I suggest rather that to remain academically viable the ethnic programs will need to balance the immediately practical with other aims.

Diversity in the society, which explains the proliferation of ethnic programs in universities, also feeds the immediate problems of their growth. A common culture seems possible to a society with branches but not to one that is all splinters, a porcupine with the needles turned inward. For all failures to restore a common culture, Cornel West blames market forces primarily for "*de facto* segregation by political persuasion, race, and subculture in a balkanized society; it is sustained by suspicion of common vocabularies or bridge-building nomenclatures."[26] That analysis, when examined, means that the vocabularies of academic multicultural suspicion sustain external market forces. However that may be, a common marketplace for ideas is a greater need than a common culture. We could achieve commonalty without dissolving constituent cultures. Without the mounting fears that diversity is an urban blight, the increase in educational ethnicity would probably be applauded generally as an improvement in higher education.

Like belief that drug addiction in the United States is a problem of laxity in policing borders, belief that urban blight and ethnicity are interchangeable terms will continue to draw the attention of journalists to multicultural programs in educational institutions. Consequently, to whatever extent diversity is a flaw that shreds the Star-Spangled Banner, educational programs in ethnicity will contribute to national disarray with distinctive characteristics locally. To the concealed or open delight of administrators, it will weaken the franchise of traditional departments and create an interregnum in faculty structures.

Higher education, which has passively increased the number of electives, has not been a leader in cultural diversity. Foresight has not been among the idiosyncrasies recently of academic leaders. For thirty-odd years, most student groups that have stated their desires as a demand have been offered a compromise that creates a new elective, sometimes a single course, sometimes a divergent path to a bachelor's degree. One raw fact is that faculties, divided by their own diversity and lacking intellectual leadership from regents, trustees, or administrators for so long that they would not accept it if it had a miraculous birth, have come to believe, not from theory but from nasty experience, that the young give more thought to large issues than any but sociological theorists and astronomers, and more thought to immediate issues than their professors in traditional disciplines.

In very few colleges do any of the ethnic and gender programs replace a core; they expand further the nationwide elective lack-of-system. The tendency has not been to form ethnic departments but to create "programs" and "studies" that draw expertise from established but diverse departments. Stanford experimented with a choice of two paths for the undergraduate: one Western, one non-Western—a divisive rather than integrating project. The repentant change at Stanford to a program in general education that includes Cultures, Ideas, and Values (area 1) and World Cultures, American Cultures, and Gender Studies (area 4) has been found by conservers equally indulgent. The three-quarter sequence of "ancient Greek philosophers," "early Christian thinkers," and "Renaissance dramatists," as a replacement for Bible, Plato, Augustine, Machiavelli, Rousseau, and Marx, has been described as the "politically correct" appointment of "delegates of certain constituencies."[27] But the Stanford program has made a good linkage of culture and values both with writing and critical thinking and with various arts. It takes significant steps toward a program in "liberal arts" that integrates, as in Integrated Liberal Studies at the University of Wisconsin, verbal, visual, and numerical thought and expression.

Multiculturists have been blamed for exacerbating a problem that had in fact begun in the earliest grades of public education. In the view of middle-range conservatives, attempts to civilize children by overlaying prejudice with tolerance have been so successful that the brighter pupils in junior high subordinate moral judgment to relativistic uncertainty. Where are prosecutors to excavate for jurors if the idea of justice gives way to Hamlet's question, "Use every man after his desert, and

who shall scape whipping?" or Sir William Blackstone's adage, "It is better that ten guilty persons escape than that one innocent suffer"? Will
not a student of cultures including Aztec come to embrace ritual murder and a student of Hindu to accept suttee? The problem of moral relativism needs to be genuinely addressed, but a problem ceases to seem
real when exaggerated as in John Leo's "A No-Fault Holocaust," where
belief in animal rights is treated as a fuzziness concerning ritual (or
mass) murder.[28] Isaiah Berlin in 1960, more philosophically than Irving
Babbitt in 1919, identified the rise of relativism, "the destruction of the
notion of truth and validity in ethics and politics, not merely objective
or absolute truth, but subjective and relative truth also," as beginning in
the Romanticism of the late eighteenth century.[29] It is less the relativism of the multicultural than the political impetus and aims of vocal
multiculturalists that excite opposition.

The effectiveness of aims that are objectionable to half the campus
has resulted from institutional drift. Why oppose these aims with political afterthought but not educationally? Have institutions or faculties
frightened by the relativism of the multicultural considered how interested undergraduates would be in general colloquia on moral judgments and moral decisions? Has the secular left made universities fear
the risks of judgment and the sectarian right made it impossible for
teachers to distinguish between religion and moral choice? It certainly
looks as if the religious right has frightened colleges into questioning
the wisdom of courses in the Bible as literature. In courses either of literature or of cultures, teachers worried by relativism could assign
works from the vast library of fiction and drama involving moral
choice and ask students hard questions about those choices. Plutarch
used to be taught with that purpose in mind.

Practical objections to multiculturist schemes come as a package:
new programs could increase institutional costs; added electives dilute
the curriculum; ethnic studies seem to result, not from diverse needs in
a diverse society but from abandoning rational standards to student
will. In truth, though, ethnic studies cannot be freed from debates over

immigration and global commerce; if they were merely an academic phenomenon, they would fade away.

Meanwhile, *meanwhile*, higher education compromises between financial considerations and fear of unrest. If a new program draws fewer students per class meeting than the institutional average, without a compensating factor of lower-paid teachers, the additional cost will receive serious study. (A new program will also increase costs if the administration decides that it requires additional administrators.) If a new program attracts enough students to require additional faculty (initially in most schools lecturers or adjuncts), then the next budget will call for a reduction in the faculty of already weakened departments. In this way, for three centuries, colleges in the United States have been transformed, a gradual evolution with intermittent intensifications.

Inevitably, the emphases in ethnic and cultural studies will vary from one sector of the country to another. Institutions in California have a greater number of ethnic programs than most, as a penalty California pays for growing oversized fruit and vegetables that need tending, being the edge beyond which native Americans could not be pushed, and providing a suitable base for Goldwyn and Disney. Universities in Oklahoma now teach Cherokee. Chicano studies will seldom attract or serve students, or stimulate important research, in an area where Jewish studies other than biblical were the first in the current wave to be introduced. Without, however, just such alertness to changing consciousness a century and a half ago, English would not have become a department or an academic subject. Publishers and theater proprietors made Shakespeare popular before he became an academic subject.

The whole nation is served now by the attention in cultural programs to transformations, border crossings, the leveling of barriers. In cultural studies, only theory, history, and anthropology can be reliably academic, but the sociology of gender and ethnic issues in literary arts can confront, as literary study had ceased to confront, the reality of individual and collective life. Within cultural studies the student can contemplate in a single course Poussin's *Rape of Europa*, Hardy's *Tess of the d'Urbervilles*, graphic or photographed rape projected on screens of various sizes, and rape in the alley or at the back of a school bus. Literature retains a foothold here.

Some teachers of literature, sharing the aims of cultural diversity but thinking it simpler and safer to collect pertinent materials into established departments of English, have proposed abandonment of the canon and the Norton anthology, abolition of the survey course, and benign neglect of major figures; in sum, replacing anthology, survey, canon, and authors for the purpose of studying problems of particular groups at particular times in particular places.[30] Those steps will not be taken universally soon. Even so, under the prevailing theories and practices of chaos, students in traditional literary programs should have at least the option of taking courses prepared by multiculturists for diversity; multiculturists in English departments should be among those required or shepherded to pass examinations with questions on the Spenserian stanza, litotes in Shakespeare, and chiasmus in Donne, if not on the religious opinions of George Herbert.

An attempt within literary study to heal the breach between language-centered theory and concern for the environment by quashing esoteric abstraction has led since the 1970s to ecocriticism, including ecological literary criticism. Einar Haugen, in *The Ecology of Language* (1972) called for "the study of interactions between any given language and its environment," ending linguistic "seclusion in the library."[31] Ecological exploration stemming from Haugen and from Gregory Bateson's *Steps to an Ecology of Mind* (1972) has led, as in the scholarship of James C. McKusick, to a rediscovery of vitality in etymological derivation and neologisms. Conservers of tradition may well make a more specifically environmental approach to literature and language their next target, so healthful has the attempt been to seize "opportunities offered by recent biological research to make humanistic studies more socially responsible."[32] A department of Geology can quietly change its name to Earth and Environmental Sciences, but a department of English that becomes Earth and the Literature of Humanity will attract wasps. Meanwhile, change in literary study can be expected to resemble the loss of refreshing ozone by global warming more than annihilation by an asteroid. True, a literary environmentalist incurs not only the charge but also a temptation of "a holier-than-thou ecological self-righteousness."[33] Even so, ecological criticism offers as an example a more promising path to significance than most other current approaches. It offers a variation on the step toward filling the chasm between the aesthetic and the political defined as sociological in T*he Possibilities of Society* by Regina Hewitt (1997).

But why, the disgruntled ask, in the cause of current interest drop the requirement of accredited masterworks from traditional departments? Insisting that they understand why in a multicultural society there might be occasional courses on women in ethnic American literature and on Native American oral literatures, the disgruntled ask why, in a division that no longer requires any reading of Shakespeare, space is afforded for George Lamming and Malcolm X, neither of them as morally stringent as Milton. As for catastrophe here, it has been a very long time since a notable percentage of colleges required of any except majors in English a course devoted to Shakespeare; and most still require of underclassmen an acquaintance with bits of Shakespeare, a tragedy, a history, a comedy, in one course or another, with more than these bits on the table for the taking. With current attempts to get a large percentage of the population through college, we need English teachers who recognize in Shakespeare a very great playwright and superlative humanist but who have larger aims than forcing every student through *Love's Labor's Lost* and *Coriolanus*. Shakespeare can reasonably be thought the greatest writer who ever lived, but there are other important, accessible writings, and more will come into being each year, to aid in the task of civilizing "young barbarians all at play." The election of Toni Morrison over Shakespeare is not as subversive or as startling today as the election of Shakespeare over Cicero would have been in the seventeenth century. Harvard and Yale no longer expect every student admitted to become a political leader or major landholder, but they hope to matriculate, among others, future leaders capable of electing an arduous course of study. Locke and Jefferson, godfathers of all this, believed in freedom of election as well as in real property. What the nation currently needs is students capable of electing a course in Shakespeare. As for the incapable others, it is the opposite of wittiness to say that the surest way to make a subject leaden is to require it. Before condemning a particular multiversity, it should be remembered that most of the voting faculty there endured only one college course in literature and that one under protest. Some professors with a vote on curricula had a first cavity filled forty or fifty years ago and in this utilitarian nation were subjected to no literary garbage after high school. The majority have had fewer years to share the same freedom from imaginative uses of language. In this society it never occurred to such, unless lately, that future leaders in business, industry, or engineering might be improved by listening to teachers who mentioned *Hamlet*, *The Merchant of Venice*, or ethics.

For majors in English, independent colleges and moderately sized universities have no trouble making Shakespeare prominent among the courses available. Nostalgic parents fretting because offspring could choose the freely elective major in English at Penn State rather than the more restrictive honors there might prefer Wisconsin, where Shakespeare and one other course before 1800 are required of majors (including those in the School of Education), or UCLA, where courses in Chaucer as well as Shakespeare are required, or Stanford, where Shakespeare and courses in every period from medieval to contemporary are, for the major, required. Or a traditional college such as Reed. Or the numerous community colleges where preparatory courses include unassailable works of literature.

Albeit Jefferson and Harvard's Eliot failed to demolish rigidity, options have been in place a long time; some objectors for whom Shakespeare is the shibboleth simply can't bear Maya Angelou and Toni Morrison as electives, though the feminism of such literary gems as

Ursula LeGuin's short short story on Eve's unnaming of the animals might make that riposte to Adam equally suspect. The rule that nothing new should be admitted without challenge is not likely to fade away unnoticed. After the requirement of particular British authors replaced under challenge the mandatory Latin and Greek, the next challenge to the challengers came with the introduction of American literature, of Emerson and Thoreau, as elective alternates. Diversity of perspectives and cultures has not come as a revolution: "Change," observed Disraeli, "is constant."

In a major irony of American culture, creative and inventive persons and their sympathetic publicists convince others of like or susceptible mind that they carry perpetual American progress to new heights, while greater numbers lament each innovation that tosses surviving fragments of the vision of Madison, Hamilton, and the Adams family into an abyss of landfill. Such is the American condition; to avoid accepting inevitable compromise, Trotskyites leap over the perpetual muddle to join ultraconservatives, but change, compromise, and muddle win in the nation and its academies. Another characteristic of academies holds here also: the offerings and requirements in literature within four-year colleges and universities has remained relatively stable despite criers of apocalypse.[34]

Besides some major advantages of diversity, there are minor academic benefits. The gender and ethnic studies of multiculturalism create a multiplicity that assures large departments of not being divided into only two factions. In another benefit, the custodians of the humanities no longer suffer so totally from public neglect. Readjustment of the canonical within the humanities has roused conservatives outside the academy to wrath over something other than the relativistic permissiveness of allowing linguistic forms that William Safire condemns. Such organs of opinion as the *Wall Street Journal* denounce the "academic folly" of Marxist, Freudian, existentialist, deconstructivist, and uncanonical "postmodern" multiculturism. Roger Kimball and Hilton Kramer give periodic reports in the *New Criterion* on the follies and crimes of the Modern Language Association. *Newsweek* sits up when the London *Times Literary Supplement* calls attention to the "masturbatory reading" of Dickens in *Sex Scandal: The Private Parts of Victorian Fiction* by William A. Cohen of the University of Maryland.[35] Scott Heller, in *ARTnews*, notes the contagion of a new field: "One of those everything-and-nothing terms that gets academics excited, visual culture has become an umbrella for scholars in art history, film studies, social history, literature, philosophy—and even optical science." His article carries an all-caps heading: "The Once Insurgent Methods— Marxism, Feminism, Gay and Lesbian Theory, Semiotics, and Now 'Visual Culture'—Are Firmly Part of the Academic Mainstream."[36] Representatively, John L'Heureux's novel *The Handmaid of Desire* divides its English department into old Fools and young Turks, including, of course, believers in "theory and discourse" as well as representatives of women's, lesbians', gays', Marxists', Foucauldians', chicanos', and other such causes. The "of course" in the previous sentence memorializes an editorial in the *Wall Street Journal* foreseeing disaster in the departure of Joseph Epstein from the *American Scholar*:

> A piece had to have a bit of tone and wit, carry a hint, at least, of intellectual rigor and be, not least, eminently readable. This standard, *of course*, excluded most of the politicized "studies" done by partisans of the new Cultural Revolution in English and Humanities departments all over the land [italics added].[37]

Journalists began to condemn academic focus on text in the 1930s exactly when teachers in the humanities began to gaze off the page into current conditions of American life. It is unlikely that teachers of literature, taken as a lump, will become acceptable to columnists who respect property equally with persons, who find family values absent from a course in the sociology of the family (not to speak of the sociology of sex roles) but present in a promise of fidelity to a third wife, who equate the ethnic with disintegration, who declare the governments of Europe morally culpable for lending financial support to the arts.

Shields have clashed in a twilight from dusk to dark. As teachers in social studies did in the 1950s, humanists "consider themselves an occupational minority toward which significant sectors of the community hold relatively contemptuous attitudes."[38] Students of literature should have been invited to join the discussion of journalists, lawyers, and public officials in the duPont Forum, at Columbia University early in 1997, on "How we got the public to hate us." Luckily for teachers, a notable portion of those who hate Congress but reelect their representatives are also those who oppugn the overestimated powers of college faculties but exchange memories of a caring teacher of composition or Spanish who enhanced life.

Unfortunately, the Jeane Kirkpatricks and Camille Paglias can hit a two-headed bird with one stone. Gender and ethnic studies have contrived to awaken objections from outside the academy by seeking intellectual distinction through the self-enclosing language and methodologies of deconstructive theory. In May 1997 the Associated Press, typically, was able to circulate a gleeful story that jargon-hunters in New Zealand had awarded to prominent English professors the top prizes for academic replacement of English with jargon. One need not claim the moral heights of a Roger Kimball or William Bennett, or the prescience of John Searle, to lament the distance academic custodians of literature have put between themselves and a potential public. The putative custodians continue to answer, "We can't explain ourselves or our subject to you." One recent example, from a scholar under challenge from the chairman of a state board of higher education, therefore one in a position to strangle the whole system: "I don't think Mr. Carlin understands the essential connection between teaching and research. I'm an editor of a journal called *Theater Topics*. That requires a lot of very hard, interdisciplinary work, but how can I explain that to him?"[39]

Congressmen, legislators, and their constituents have their own uncorrected ideas of the multicultural. Given the national mood, it is perhaps not odd that opponents of cultural studies include administrators who have previously lamented the intransigence of departments in resisting integrated, interdisciplinary, and elective programs.

Indeed, if in a small, independent college a newly created program in Asian studies can now mean Asian-American, in a large university intellectual collaboration, influenced by the multicultural, can now be obtained separately from Latin, Greek, and classics in such programs as classical culture, classical humanities, and classical civilization, drawing upon political, architectural, scientific, and other histories, including traditional philosophy. Such programs are what modern ethnic programs can become. Whatever the motives for forming an ethnic scheme, it must rest on more than aspiration to be academic. If only a Chicana has the knowledge initially to teach a given course, the knowledge must be communicable; a subject that only one with experience as a Chicana could teach is not academic. Whatever their future, the most academically praiseworthy aspect of ethnic studies so far is their interdisciplinarity.

What deserves rebuke in literary and cultural studies today is the fragmentation—a seriocomic scenario in which sodden firefighters spray water on each other while the house burns down. Although literary scholars of the variety dominant in the 1930s are now a minority, they remain the largest single "school" in academic literary study. Other schools share little besides rejection of traditional scholarship as emblematic of authority. Amidst the cacophony, self-preservation requires correlated searches, inward from the circumference, for a common core.

The triennial meetings of the International Association of University Professors of English began in the 1950s with one session in the morning on literature and one on language, then a second session on each in the afternoon, with free discussion in groups as small as two in the hours between sessions and before an address in the evening. The Modern Language Association (of the United States and Canada) had not been that elitist since the 1890s, nor had it been that hopeful of finding common ground. It did, however, have a habit of honoring seniority only slightly less systematic than that of the U. S. Senate. The planned revolution in the Modern Language Association at the annual meeting of 1968 brought needed democratization and greatly enlarged opportunity for the young to be heard. Several varieties of discontent gave an effective nudge to the inertia of custom. An organization of somnolent seniors presiding over ranks and files of slowly, steadily advancing youth, with a job market at its circumference, became a congeries in which academic specialties of language, period, and genre became subdivided and reduplicated.

Cross-breeding spawned what biologists had not witnessed: new species having freedom to explore but unable to mate with each other. Many older professors, by withdrawing from membership or ceasing to attend meetings, made way for the underemployed. Without the advantage enjoyed by Congress of two hostile parties, democratization of the MLA has afforded self-determination to many small groups that can ignore each other.

What has ensued not only enables Marxists, feminists, Sassurians, Lacanists, Ricoeurists, Bakhtinists, biographers, New Historicists, classicists, Romantics, gays, lesbians, whateverists to design sessions and encourages individualists to do their own thing (which may be especially enlightening), but the plenitude of sessions allows such groups to arrange a program of two and a half days such that they need listen only to each other and speak only to the converted. Meantime, such publishers on general problems of education as Jossey-Bass and Addison-Wesley are not listed in *PMLA*'s Directory of Useful Addresses.

In 1947, with a membership of five thousand and almost half that many in attendance, the annual meeting of the Modern Language Association in Detroit had 59 sections and groups and 62 sessions altogether. At the meeting of 1965 there were 65 sections and groups and 108 sessions, including 40 conferences. The general topics were Phonetics, Bibliographic Evidence, Literature and Society, Literature and Science, Literature and Other Arts, Literature and Psychology. In 1975, after democratization, there were about 410 sessions, including 344 seminars.

(The subject of Seminar 344 was "Teaching Shakespeare"; the innovative Forum 5 was on "Women Writers of the West Coast.") In 1996 there were 747 sessions, extending from 8:30 A.M. to 10:15 P.M. on two full days, with 138 sessions from 8:30 A.M. to 3 P.M. on the last day. In 1997 membership had grown to thirty-one thousand, but for twenty-five years or more planning has frequently needed to assume as many as ten thousand in attendance, many of them involved less in the sessions than in the hiring process (at the job center and in institutional hotel rooms and suites). In 1997, at Toronto, the number of sessions had stabilized at 745, with more old-fashioned pedantry and with agreement on at least one twentieth-century theme: though lacking identities or persistent personalities, we all have sharable bodies.

MLA celebrates annually our diaspora. The appropriate response to all in this agglomeration of cliques, each laying claim to a uniform certainty, whether ironic deconstructionists, Iserian audience responders, Marxian historicists, Marxian culturists, or gender cultists, is that of God in Swift's squib "The Day of Judgement," addressing all sects that had "come to see each other damn'd"—"Go, go, you're bit." The changes, with chronological, methodological, linguistic, ethnic, and sexual crisscrossing, have come less from policy than from acceptance of demand. A coherent policy would encourage a search for common ground.

The crying need is not to eliminate diversity but to discover and promulgate what scholars and critics of language and literature have yet in common, preferably something other than the instinct of self-preservation. Common interest has become so unexpected that Eudora Welty was assigned a space (in Chicago, 1990) so much too small that opening a second room to extend her voice electronically did not accommodate the overflow that wished to hear her. Welty's "Why I Live at the P.O." is one of the few things that members of the MLA know they have in common. They do hold in common world literature, vaguely considered, and for most with tenure TIAA-CREF pension insurance. The outward turn toward ethnic studies has not perceptibly reduced the strife for distinction that brings recognition to a few but makes humanists seem a single class only to distant observers, observers who have chosen distance. Humanists threaten to replicate a Texas myth: Thermopylae had its messenger; the Alamo had none. It will take more than a messenger to save the fort.

Persons speaking for the Modern Language Association have begun to express the desire to convince a larger audience of their bona fides. It will not be effective to say to conservatives, "I have embezzled the literary heritage of your children for their own good." It will be necessary to say what that good is. Deconstructionists have not meant to say that deconstructive literary study is an instability lacking determinable value. The moment for finding common ground is now, when the public media are paying attention to literary study, when columnists and "hosts" turn, for several moments at a time, from political scandals to indict a discomposed body of teachers who, if not innocent, are ineffective, which in social affairs is the equivalent of innocence. It serves the advance of science that we do not have a third of the schools trying to do mathematics with roman numerals or notches on trees. Literary study is not comparably fortunate. If professors of literature and language were divided equally between proponents of multiculturism and their opponents, the case might forbid immediate action; as we do not have two blocks, but instead a waste barrel from splintering, inert mutual tolerance can with effort become a dedicated front. Women have an opportunity to take a dominant role in whipping the MLA into cohesion somewhere near the top. Cohesion is the curse word that should echo annually in the hotels half-priced because nobody else wants their rooms December 27th to 30th. The MLA should convene a conference on comprehensive literary study in which the subtitle of each paper would be, "Aims and Ideas I Hold in Common with All Others Invited to Speak at This Conference."

Under publicized conditions, enrollments in the humanities have been declining. External funds for research have been diverted from the humanities. Full-time teachers of literature diminish annually. Some 36 percent of colleges and universities have no requirements in literature; only 20 percent require a single specific course in literature.[40] Whatever their degree of blame, teachers of literature have many reasons for concern.

Revolutionary comradeship will not save departments of literature. We need a collaborative rather than a collective future. Humanists cannot argue successfully with a person convinced that American and European social and intellectual structures should be destroyed; there are not at present enough such persons to bring those structures down, but if all the enemies of English departments found each other, a small beginning could be made.

Economists and political scientists have good reason for regarding their humanistic colleagues as supremely unaware. No less frequently buffeted and battered by economic forces than individuals otherwise employed, academic humanists have been consistently aware only of the nearest external context of all college and university teaching and research: the nonteaching administrative bureaucracy—the moat that begins the surround.

CHAPTER FIVE

The Surround

Professors in the humanities cannot send a bill to students they have scheduled for a conference. Professors of literature and language will not need to launder money gained from professional advice for privatizing in another country; nor can they extract large consulting fees locally. Otherwise, the conditions of their employment strike most observers as highly enviable. In addition to the holidays others celebrate, those under a scheduling system of two semesters have at least a week off from classes and examinations near the end of the calendar year, another week when the students take a spring break, and nearly three months in those summers when financial status may allow relief from summer teaching. The larger universities are likely to afford sabbaticals or research leaves of a half or, combined with grants, a full year. Except for rapid preparation and cover for a colleague fallen ill or accused of malfeasance, emergencies seldom increase or interrupt the expected schedule of professors in the humanities, and humanists do not, like research biologists and ballet dancers, risk disaster by interrupting routine for a day. Furthermore, very few stand in crowded classrooms as often as the sixteen hours a week common until the 1950s; a graduate teacher responsible for the supervision of dissertations and for oral and other examinations outside the classroom, and expected to continue a record of honored publications, might have the enjoyment of only four, or two, hours a week "in class." That a privileged few teach less, or never, did not find its source in a teachers' union. Only great courage, rare humility, or administrative fiat will lead professors to invite into their department a distinguished outsider with the promise of minimal teaching and no committees.

Most professors regard themselves as always pressed for time, usually as driven to the edge of exhaustion. What they like best about the schedule is that so little of it is under the tyranny of a clock. They dislike the restraints of only twenty-four hours in each day and the threat that a total lack of sleep brings death. They are busy professionally on the weekends, into the night, throughout the summers. They regard as the genuinely enviable aspect of the profession, other than fellowship with minds of rich harvest and those beginning to ripen, the freedom to choose—that is, to shuffle variously—most of the hours for doing what they have to do.

What then, is it that professors in the humanities do in all those hours? In brief, they search out the optimum sources for achieving and maintaining mastery of the chosen or assigned field; prepare for classes and examinations; read, correct, and make suggestions of grammar, syntax, organization, expression, and thought on themes, essays, theses, dissertations, and exam papers of students; serve on departmental, divisional, and institutional committees that require investigation, reports, and an iron bottom; listen to each other at professional meetings; assess students for departmental purposes and for higher authority; compose letters of recommendation; read and pronounce judgment on books and articles because administrations of other universities demand outside assessments of teachers proposed by their own departments for appointment; and, in endless expanse, conduct research as interpreters, theorists, translators, biographers, historians, bibliographers analytic or comprehensive, or, for a few, research as educators. The best pause to think; most, like pursued rabbits, think on the run.

At a midwestern university where a requirement was introduced that faculty members keep a diary of activities and submit it for review, we began to keep hourly records and then consulted with each other about the alarming evidence that we each spent at least sixty hours a week in job-related activity. An exact determination was difficult; a diary could show seventy hours when in fact several tumultuous consultations that week had subsided gradually into gossip: professors paid to talk and write find it difficult to stop talking. Later, in New York, I found that professors living farthest from the city, with its lecturing, consultation, committees, and conversation, had the best chance of making the requirement of research the only intrusion into something like private pursuits on weekends. Some preserved a modicum of family life by grading papers on the train. A few given to drink, but no golfers. A survey of 1988 found that faculty at public doctoral universities averaged fifty-four to fifty-seven hours a week at institutional or professional work.[1]

Why research? For three centuries, and increasingly, the nation has depended upon universities (originally colleges) for almost all basic scientific research and for a large proportion of all scientific and social research. Research in universities has been the most nearly disinterested, the most open to any possibility, of exploration anywhere. In humanistic tasks of conserving the heritage and exploring the possibilities of effective change, almost all investigation has been accomplished within college and university faculties. With the progressive reduction of financial aid to humanistic scholars from private foundations, the National Endowment for the Humanities became a crucial source of support for scholars hoping to afford leave for research. A large portion of humanistic research now continues unsupported except for the institutional requirement of publication. Bits of the finest research in libraries, as distinguished from laboratories, has been conducted by independent scholars; with other responsibilities and a scarcity of financial support, their numbers have been few.

Unlike major projects in medical and physical sciences, research by team has been rare in the humanities, but production of scrupulous editions of major authors, of the sort that led to the Library of America, would have ceased without support from the NEH and private foundations for editors in the academy, and some, requiring innovative networking computer programs, would never have begun. So completely expected in the humanities is a single individual contriving a proposal that most committees assessing research in the humanities have not known how to judge collaborative teams. How, it is asked, can a team be *original*? David Damrosch, for one, has called for institutional funding of collaborative research, a proposal doubly significant if it leads to educational collaboration between and among departments "on related issues from differing perspectives."[2] Increased cooperation, but collaboration also, are in order. Collaborative research through internetting and E-mail can increase both alertness and efficiency, but it decreases the potential of warm-breath relations across disciplines on a single campus.

It can be asked what social need a book of academic criticism serves, and luckily it is impossible to know how public libraries, academic publishers, bookstores, and purveyors on-line would fare if the humanities were dropped from higher education, but there is some evidence that it is chiefly academic scholarship, including critical discourse, that kept humanistic literature flowing as a stream through the twentieth century. Careful reading supported by careful search through manuscripts, proofs, and printings, and careful research into contexts, producing a progression of corrective assertions, has brought syntheses that have been too seldom explained for a wider audience. Academic humanists have lost the readers who can, for example, learn from Helen Vendler a reason for reading lyric poetry—when led by public reviewers to her clear analyses of Shakespeare's sonnets.

The *requirement* of publication has nourished both mediocrity and opacity. It has greater crimes on its head. In a thoughtful administrator's assessment, "teaching loads have grown lighter, absences from campus more frequent, and commitments to outside activities more substantial—although . . . administrative demands and the institution's own reward structure bear some of the responsibility."[3] "Some of the responsibility" means, in the words of another, that administrators have "shunted the teacher types off to limbo" and have indulged a "somewhat informal annual page count" for publications of their own faculty.[4] Even the Internal Revenue Service has been brought to distinguish between the costs of improving one's conditions of employment and a professor's costs of research as a requirement of the position held. Faculties have not been primarily responsible in recent decades for the growth in universitywide research. Even among community colleges, particularly those belonging to a citywide "system," some require publication for advancement.

Research for publication can be creative. As teachers have generally chosen the subjects for study, emphasis on research to uncover the sexual preferences and indiscretions of minor poets of fourteenth-century Silesia understandably alarms the governors of education, but the institutionalization of research would be hard to replace with an equal safeguard of quality. Teachers inspired by the chase after innovative knowledge are teachers to have.

Judgment by peers in a small institution cannot, and in universities does not, mean judgment by immediate colleagues. The president and deans hope to discover how specialists qualified to know regard present and prospective members of their faculty. For the recruitment of superior students, they wish to proclaim their high reputation relative to competing institutions. Faculty and alumni agree on the importance of reputation. If as alumna I give $5 million to my alma mater in support of research, I will be thought to have gone to a better college than you may previously have thought I did.

Most superior teachers have not found onerous the institutional requirements of publication. That published research achieves reputation outside the narrow range of hearsay about teaching serves the individual researcher as well as the institution. Most professors would rather examine intensely a favorite topic than mark blue books. Pride is better fed by exposing the errors of other specialists than correcting an annoying grammatical error for the twentieth year and thousandth time. The professor on research leave has broken free of schedule and committees. Emphasis on publication invites rival institutions to compete in salary and perquisites for the faculty names most widely known. Despite these enticements, the premium on research owes its universality to administrators, not faculty. With standards of productivity set in the sciences, administrations ask for equivalent demonstrations of productivity from departments that rely on words for existence. The department that recommends for tenure a spectacularly dedicated and successful teacher (or one with glazed eyes from excessive service on committees) is systematically defeated on the grounds that personality cannot be weighed against productivity. Some administrations reduce argument by erecting a simple standard: no second book, no tenure.

Nothing in this discussion should be taken as a pretence that faculties will cheerfully abandon the reductions in course preparation, classroom attendance, and marking of papers and examination books that administrative emphasis on research has bestowed upon them. The spirit dampened by large classes with objective examinations can be refreshed by a sense of creative endeavor in a booklined cubby. Emphasis on research has promoted the overemphasis on the Ph.D. degree as the only acceptable qualification for permanence as a college teacher; reductions in course load go to PhDs as productive researchers. Most professors in the humanities remember that they entered graduate school as a choice to accept the responsibilities and low pay of those who excite the young to love of knowledge, not to add to the plethora of articles in scholarly journals. One of the brightest colleagues I have known, the Shakespearean S. F. Johnson, a meticulous scholar, proposed in a Swiftian mood that the university establish a scale of reductions in salary for every article or book published. One who has served as a university executive concludes that "outstanding scholar-teachers will never receive tenure at 'research institutions' unless top administrators recognize that research is a network of activities whose success and quality are not determined solely by what ends up between the covers of a journal or book."[5]

Departments vote often not to recommend tenure or initial appointment of a superior but unpublished teacher, because they know that both the recommendation and the person recommended would be without future in that institution. Indeed, more often than anyone admits, a researcher who can go elsewhere on the basis of publication is not recommended by the department for tenure because demonstrably an irresponsible or natively incompetent teacher. And prominent senior professors have been cheerfully bade farewell because they have shunned teaching and committees. But a department knows collectively that the administration will allocate funds on the basis of departmental renown from public or professional reviews of its published research. Departments have engaged in self-congratulation for tolerance when they vote to retain an abhorred colleague who enhances the departmental reputation for productivity.

Universities, most of all the overarching bodies that administer state systems of higher education, recklessly requisition the time of each other's faculties for "outside opinions," necessarily based on published research and performance at conferences rather than on teaching and other service to the institution that wants to know. In a typical case, a superior scholar I had sponsored as a graduate student, but had not seen for nine years, taught at a prominent state university that asked me in seven years of the nine to comment on his rate of progress: for renewal of contract, for a summer grant, for committees, for tenure, for graduate teaching. Any comment to the effect that the institution has had years of opportunity to observe, as the consultant has not, would be registered as a negative judgment on the candidate. Solicited letters are scrutinized for evidence of reluctance to declare this candidate foremost in the field. Time spent on assessments and reviews of performance of colleagues could be better invested in teaching, for example by replacing inflated grades with individualized assessments of students.

Harvard's system of convening an ad hoc committee of experts to advise on a prospective appointment to tenure has frequently included, among those convened, professors who find the candidate merely adequate because less remarkably fitted for this position than each of them is. How would you rank this candidate with Sir Isaiah Berlin? With Sir Frank Kermode? With Northrop Frye or Erich Auerbach or Julia Kristeva? Has she been observed turning water into wine? If so, how many times? Such questions are not asked when administrators have chosen the candidate.

My gratitude for generous retirement benefits is slightly tempered by suspecting that each costly fringe benefit for all seniors emerged from bidding wars over distinguished persons of high profile. At one moment half the elite institutions compete for the same eminent woman or theorist or African American or digital whiz with little benefit to instruction and only secondary benefit to less eminent members of the respective groups. Students and their parents who fret that few of the diminishing numbers of tenured professors teach first-year students should worry a great deal more about management's device, as one way of offsetting the cost of the most wanted, of providing students as "customers" or "products" with inexperienced temporary or part-time adjuncts who will not accumulate salary increases by continuity on the job.

If few professors can become the peripatetic equivalent of best sellers, and administrators erect more stringent requirements for publication than those proposed by faculties in the humanities, why can persons who regarded their entrance into graduate school as a consecration to the ministry be overheard saying as teachers, "I can't find time for my own work"? By "own work" they mean what you thought they meant, study and writing for publication, and what you may not have remembered they would mean, the requirement for advance in salary and rank as a major part of the understood contract for continuance. Fortunately, also, most have come to find greater pleasure in steadily increased intellectual breadth and depth than in repeating, or repeatedly polishing, tricks that please students. In the humanities keeping up with current developments is more psychic refreshment than intellectual necessity, but what most of us have always preferred to believe has been demonstrated experimentally: even at the extreme end of tenure, meeting intellectual challenge modifies the physical brain.

What is the alternative to judgment of published research by peers? The danger, at least, of Mr. Chipps cloned. Any group satisfied with its own interests and methods suffers the temptation to perpetuate those methods and interests. The president of a small college makes all appointments to the faculty because she knows that each departmental clan would replicate its own kind if allowed to choose successors. To replace "publish or perish" with "read or perish" is easy to recommend.[6] Reading what? Research in the humanities has already become largely reading what others are propounding about what still others have propounded or questioned. Besides works of literature, teachers in the humanities need most to read far outside their fields, to try books recommended in the *Scientific American*, perhaps, more often than those reviewed in the *Smithsonian*. A strong effort to enlarge the humanistic center has been maintained by the periodical *Common Knowledge*, edited by Jeffrey M. Perl.

Abuses of time off for research occur, but each educational institution bears the responsibility to curb malpractice by those who have carried into adulthood a tendency to substitute play or sleep for work. Shirking or other malpractice during a teacher's years of probation is easy to punish. Dismissal of a professor with tenure is, and ought to be, hard. Assessment of intellectually responsible teaching will be harder than weighing the amount of published research, but it can be done. Attention to the relation between research and tenure has led all of us to neglect the need for continuity, with or without traditional tenure, for alert teachers of composition.

If incompetence can be identified, it should be eliminated. This question has been journalistically entangled with a problem that threatens future strength in higher education, a problem for which administrators deserve sympathy: the decision of Congress to make age an unacceptable reason for termination. Tenured faculties grow older, with accumulated increases in salary and other costs, while various strata-gems are practiced administratively to avoid commitment to the young who have passed all the tests of probation.

Older tenured faculty in universities with doctoral programs have a moral responsibility to propose modifications of tenure or to plan vol-untary retirement, or to fight the current tendencies in employment, or all three. I have no conviction of guilt from mistakes made in forty years of teaching that approaches the pain of failure to secure teaching positions for outstanding young scholars whom I had helped guide to the Ph.D. degree in the present era, when the profession is a pit with the pendulum swinging. Of the thirty-one thousand members of the Mod-ern Language Association, one-third lack tenure. At Yale, which in the humanities admittedly takes more pride than most universities in slaughter, of PhDs in humanities departments hired between 1980 and 1990, 13 percent achieved tenure (compared with 53 percent in the bio-logical sciences).[7] Ignoring the concept of tenure, this means that 87 percent of the young were fired. Granting that a teacher not kept at Yale has a better chance than most of going elsewhere, it is extremely rare that the person displaced from Yale will fill a position added elsewhere for the purpose. The portion of "permanent" positions open nationally has decreased by what one might ghoulishly call leaps and bounds.

Administrations did not wait for congressional uncapping of tenure to give it leaden feet. Reduction in appointments bearing tenure began suddenly in 1970–71. Of college teachers qualified by education, experience, ability, and performance to be granted tenure, in 1970 about 92 percent achieved tenure; in 1971, about 28 percent. Percentages of those granted tenure have remained low ever since. A revolving bottom, as at Yale, along with part-time and transient employment, helps depress budgets exploding for reasons other than education. The Uni-versity of California has set a pattern for budget-cutting avoidance of employing the qualified young by "contracting out (or 'outsourcing') certain academic programs."[8] Most institutions have simply reduced the numbers of full-time, continuing teachers. In its *Final Report* of

December 1997, a courageous attempt to mitigate the sufferings of young holders of the doctorate in English or foreign languages, the MLA Committee on Professional Employment provides recent percentages: "of the 7,598 PhDs who emerged from our graduate programs in the first half of the nineties, *4,188—55%—failed in the year the degree was awarded to find the kind of employment for which they had presumably been trained*."[9]

Carol Christ of the University of California at Berkeley has recommended that departments increase the chances of preserving opened positions by entering partnerships with other departments.[10] The measures of management to reduce and if possible eliminate departmental autonomy will make easier their replacement of continuing teachers with part-time and temporary employees who have no more vested interest in the future of higher education than the current management has.

Even more money could be saved at the top. Humanists feel less fitted than those who have retired from military command to enter other gainful employment, although assistant professors trained by humanists but denied tenure began to learn in the 1970s that methods acquired in securing the Ph.D. could be applied in businesses that did no obeisance to the graduate degree earned for the purpose of tenure. We professors had a ready excuse for not retiring early in order to let the brightest serve the future in academic positions for which they were best fitted: central administrations across the nation closed faculty positions—not all, but a menacing number—vacated by retirement, departure, or death and instead appointed more assistants to vice presidents. The cost to the qualified young has been in eagerness and confidence; the cost to society has been intellectual. The cost to undergraduates has become obvious. The educational cost to undergraduates tomorrow will be greater.

By 1988, 39.4 percent of faculty nationally was over forty-nine, 21.7 percent under forty, with the discrepancy widening each year thereafter and projected to continue; already, far more are over sixty-five than under thirty-five.[11] By retaining a burdensome portion of the faculty budget, elders tacitly encourage administrators to employ part-time temporaries and others treated as untenurable, to the detriment of higher education and civilization. In four-year private colleges in 1987, as reported in the *Chronicle of Higher Education* of September 6, 1989, 48 percent of the faculty were part-time or temporary. Of a reported 526,222 full-time faculty in four-year colleges nationally in 1996, more than 241,499 lacked tenure, "more than" because not all the 123,471 associate professors had been granted tenure, nor even all of the 161,252 full professors, who, tenured or not, obscured the view from below.[12]

Oscar M. Ruebhausen has suggested the replacement of tenure by contracts covering twenty to thirty-five years, but it is not clear that the law forbidding mandatory retirement because of age allows this evasion; protection begins at age forty.[13] Schemes that would create teaching positions for a later generation ignore the immediate need. Along with voluntary early retirement, part-time teaching after sixty-five or so is a possibility that should be explored. With health, housing, and financial competence assured, a legal solution might be to superannuate professors at or before seventy into advisory or other tasks—but as administrators only if they replace two others. Shelvers of library books, operators of visual equipment, and groundskeepers accomplish more essential ends than most assistants to vice presidents. Of course Congress was on this issue correct: age can sometimes advance without senility. Experience and wisdom can accrue. Many seniors—like one eighty-five-year-old who teaches choral music without salary—have experience, talent, and commitment that will not be equaled by any younger replacement. The problem lies not in the seniors, except as they passively accept the system that now endangers the future of higher education in the United States and elsewhere.

The criterion for early retirement under the present circumstances is neither accomplishment nor reduction in competence but the national good in making room for young minds to develop and perform. Toward professors who have nourished the young through graduate school, the finger points as in war posters: volunteer now. The alternative is a fight to the death against managers. Such a fight would be honorable, for it is not in the sciences alone that "the overproduction of Ph.D.s in many disciplines results in increasingly fierce competition for both research funds and the relatively few full-time positions available."[14] The aging who stay ought to devote a large portion of their time in efforts to assure the future of intellect in higher education before the effectiveness of faculty is completely eroded by management.

Graduated retirement based on performance and perceived value belongs to a world of presidential sweet dreams. Budgets can be built on private review, to punish the ordinary and reward the fashionable; forced retirement is a stickier subject. What kind of open review of academic performance can be of genuine help to education? What kind of review can improve educational achievement within the institution? For success, any open codification of review with termination as a possibility will have to be accompanied by other terms of agreement. Review that achieves only a reduction of costs for the same number of teachers and the removal of professors who express annoying opinions will be, and should be, resisted by all who expect universities to have a significant role in the nation's future.

Review without benefit to the untenured young, and therefore to future enlightenment, will serve no healthy purpose. Even on the discouraging assumption that humanists will continue to speak only to each other, the voices of tomorrow should be the best obtainable. Universities, and the nation, should train exactly the number of humanists employable; as resolutely as the armed forces took sacrificial steps to protect and rescue trained pilots in recent wars, universities should nourish the young they have trained. Universities can best survive by a steadily continuing inflow of intellectual innovation from the young. A good idea grows stale from local repetition. In the humanities as in medicine or engineering, valuable strength within a given institution has come from adding to the faculty minds innovatively trained elsewhere. Fortunately, many estimable professors who have never left the institution they entered as freshmen have imported constructive innovation from elsewhere: a new approach to *Paradise Lost*; introduction of a recent work, as *The Waste Land* and *Harmonium* once were, worth teaching; refinements on "point of view"; a demonstration that the last edition to receive its poet's imprimatur is not therefore sacrosanct. How old was the first person to teach Joyce's *Ulysses* to an astonished class? How young the first to teach works by Derek Walcott?

No proposal for modifying tenure with a chance of enduring can go into effect instantly. With advance warning and cautious phasing, statutory tenure should perhaps end after thirty years or by age sixty or sixty-five. If the security of housing and healthcare is assured, twenty or thirty years for demonstrating one's value to an institution would preserve many of the aims of tenure and would remain a valuable resource for persons and society concerned. If senior professors accept some such scheme, few others will dissent.

Patterns exist elsewhere for guaranteeing a minimum wage at the end of a contract for full service; in higher education the amount of this minimum plus the cost of the new position at the bottom of the scale could equal the pay of the professor at the cessation of tenure. Any difference—without resembling Congress claiming to balance a budget—could easily be met by reducing the exorbitant costs of administration.

The paramount purpose of tenure, preservation of academic freedom for the benefit of society, could be largely achieved by guaranteeing twenty or thirty years of freedom to reach an unpopular conclusion, with the chief threat, as now, of a frozen salary and reduced perks. Perhaps entirely different modifications from those suggested here will prove superior. Anyone who has a better idea for creating openings for the young, and thus windows to the future, other than dynamiting buildings full of managers, is invited to replace modification of tenure or early retirement with the better idea. If our society could be described as intelligent, tenure would be retained without change, but it is far more important to assure the entry of young minds into the teaching hierarchy of higher education than to assure unchanged conditions for autumnal professors.

Meanwhile, professors with a generous turn of mind might consider asking former students who did not achieve teaching posts how they prepared for the positions they now hold in business. Too many of us in literary study have written books with minuscule or no royalties because they were addressed to a minuscule audience; do such publications really represent the limit of our talents? The young provide a reason to test the adage, Those who can, do; those who can't, teach.

To consider modifications of tenure differs entirely from any thought that America would be better off without tenure. Elimination of the procedures known by the maligned word *tenure* would be almost as disastrous intellectually as elimination of the clause on freedom of speech in the first amendment to the Constitution. Academic tenure began as a way of preserving the benefits of intellectual independence in a climate of religious uniformity. The first president of Harvard, Henry Dunster, was forced out by the Overseers in 1654 for denying scriptural validity to infant baptism.[15] A decade of renewed struggle by the Harvard faculty for a degree of self-government, far less than the autonomy then enjoyed by each college faculty at Oxford and Cambridge, resulted in a permanent victory by the president and overseers in 1789.[16] Necessarily so. A college or university, as a corporation not for profit, distinguished by absence of profit from proprietary institutions, must under its charter be governed by a body of persons, trustees or regents, not receiving monetary gain from the corporation. Under the laws of the United States, no faculty can ultimately rule a true college or university. In the United States, literary study exists in an academic world created by regents or trustees and their administrative bureaucracies. That regents and trustees have often bought their way into appointment has significance for the immediate issue only because it increases the pressures against teachers who question, not infant baptism but the immaculate ascension of chief executive officers. In the 1960s it began to be assumed that the presence of token faculty or students on a governing board would not violate the law of nonprofitability and would do no serious harm to education; it certainly has not ended the dismissal of professors for misdeclared reasons.

A proposal to dismiss or restrain can originate at various levels, from a departmental colleague, a member of the board, an intermediate person or group, or, in state institutions, from beyond the board. A chief executive officer, designated as president or chancellor, needs both the consent and the confidence of the board to execute policies recommended for their approval. State universities, with or without intermediate boards and officials supervising a system of universities, are subject ultimately to the state legislature and governor. Thirty-nine states have systems intermediate between separate institutions and the government.

In 1915 the American Association of University Professors (AAUP) was founded to preserve for higher education teachers of proved intellectual distinction who espoused causes politically, socially, or religiously unpopular. Most governing boards chafing to dismiss a particular member of a faculty have begun by applying thumbscrews to the president or chancellor. Dismissal until late in the nineteenth century was usually on religious grounds; after Cornell, Stanford, Chicago, and other universities were founded by philanthropic capitalists, the grounds of dismissal became most often political. In the 1890s Mrs. Stanford asserted the necessity of dismissing professors who expressed opinions unworthy of the university that bore her husband's name and of others who supported such persons.[17] During World War I a professor was fired from a major university for petitioning Congress to exempt those unwilling to fight in Europe; in another university in 1915, where a mine owner on the board of trustees had a strong voice, a socialist professor of economics "lost his position for publicly opposing the use of child labor in coal mines."[18] Dismissals have come in waves ever since.

Between 1930 and 1967 the AAUP after investigation censured sixty-two institutions for violations of tenure by dismissal without due process.[19] Amidst a prolonged season of dismissals and maledictions at the University of Washington during the Cold War, the case of the state un-American activities committee against Melvin Rader (Professor of Philosophy, author of the basically Platonic *Presiding Ideas in Wordsworth's Poetry* and protester against dismissal and probationary status of others without due process) was proved by a reporter for the Seattle *Times* to be based on deliberately falsified evidence.[20] Noting two firings by the University of Minnesota in 1985 and 1988, Ralph S. Brown and Jordan E. Kurland remark that the firing of professors with tenure occurs "several times each year."[21]

For the precariousness of tenure among professors of German origin, and for the few of Japanese origin, an emblem remains in the group portrait of major psychologists in Emerson Hall at Harvard: a blank space stands beside William James where Hugo Münsterberg stood before the American mind confused him with Kaiser Wilhelm II. It took a new belief that Russia was the enemy for Professor Heinrich Meyer to recover his citizenship after a Department of Justice charge that he had never intended to be loyal, with consequent dismissal from Rice Institute. (He should not have let French colleagues learn that he had called French, in jest, a dead language. An active traitor, or an irresolute teacher, would have been more discreet.) Across the nation intimidation has performed more effectively than open dismissal to reduce the freedom of universities to meet their responsibility of seeking the truth. It is perhaps a benefit that few professors of literature dare say in public what they say in private.

The Statement of Principles on Academic Freedom and Tenure of 1940, signed by university presidents as well as professors, went beyond the statement of 1915 in protecting freedom of extramural activities and including economic security as a necessity for freedom of research, "indispensable to the success of an institution in fulfilling its obligations to its students and to society."[22] In a very muddy area some governing boards and administrations have insisted that the protection of academic freedom for research and teaching requires as corollary the relinquishment of rights under the first amendment to speak as with authority on subjects outside the field of protected expertise. Some administrations, more justly but with inevitable ambiguities, warn that members of the faculty speaking publicly on subjects outside their competence as scholars are not to claim authority by naming the institutional employer.

The courts have enunciated firmly the importance to universities and to society of "the right to pursue the truth unhindered," of the need to protect "scholars and teachers who believed they were attempting to advance knowledge by calling into question widely held or accepted beliefs."[23] In 1957 Chief Justice Earl Warren, for himself and justices Brennan, Black, and Douglas, with two other justices concurring, declared that "The essentiality of freedom in the community of American universities is almost self-evident. Scholarship cannot flourish in an atmosphere of suspicion and distrust."[24] (The second sentence has proved to be true prophecy.) On the point of free speech outside the field of specialization, the Supreme Court of Illinois in 1962 sustained the dismissal of an assistant professor of biology for saying that premarital intercourse among college students was not in and of itself improper.[25] More recently, groups are equally likely, with support from students and faculty who desire free speech only for their own views, to attempt intimidation into silence of professors who have made remarks that stereotype racial groups. It is dangerous enough to freedom of research that John Silber was accurate in noting that an assistant professor of biology who believed with the Russian Lysenko in the inheritance of acquired characteristics would never achieve tenure in the United States.

Tenure needs revision not elimination. The columnist George F. Will attempted in April 1997 to support an argument against tenure by citing figures indicating immobility at the University of Texas. The choice was ill-advised. For more than a century the appointed regents of the University of Texas have been more often irritated than intimidated, and have been often enraged, by the protection tenure affords to persons of annoying opinion. In 1941–44 regents who had been appointed by Governor W. Lee ("Pass the Biscuits, Pappy") O'Daniel wanted to fire whoever the person was who assigned a portion of Dos Passos's novel *U.S.A.* as secondary reading; they struck from the budget eight displeasing research projects; they demanded that the president, Homer P. Rainey, fire a socialist-sounding professor of economics and strike from the budget three assistant professors of economics who had been "discourteous" at an antilabor meeting in Dallas; demanded that he fire one confessed and one suspected homosexual, a conscientious objector, and a dean of medicine that previous regents had appointed without consultation—and were shocked that the English department had asked innocent undergraduates to read unexpurgated Shakespeare. Unsatisfied after more than three years of bickering, they fired the president.[26] It is easy today to recognize yesterday's bigotry.

J. Frank Dobie, long head of the English department in Austin, author of *Coronado's Children* and other books about the Southwest that have been in print for more than half a century, returned from a year as visiting professor of history at the University of Cambridge expecting to have his usual days off from class because of allergies. The regents, long allergic to Dobie, dismissed him. Discords were played through similarly again when a powerful regent first stripped John Silber, as dean, of the divisions of science and social studies, and in 1970 fired him because he was falsely regarded as protecting unpopular members of the faculty. Graduate students in mathematics accumulated evidence to prove the dean certainly innocent of protecting against dismissal Professor R. L. Moore, the sponsor of their dissertations— although some of Moore's colleagues had thought it time for him to go.

Nor would Will find it easy to illustrate the intellectual insignificance of tenure by searching among other state universities for one without case histories of conflict grounded in political or social opinion. Even the University of Wisconsin, with its pride in "sifting and winnowing" for truth, has come up against regents able to identify a politically unsuitable candidate for tenure. In private colleges a charge of religious or social heresy is as likely as "socialism" to be the intimidating threat.

Rules for due process for an individual charged with moral turpitude have not changed substantially since their formulation by the AAUP in 1915, and they have been in general quietly effective. (So quiet that the solution has doubtless too often permitted the condemned to find sanctuary elsewhere.) The AAUP has ceased investigation abruptly when given evidence, for example, that an ingenious professor has invented a way to eliminate student interest in his classes.

But moral turpitude becomes a public issue most often when professors interpret the Constitution and John Locke's recommendations of tolerance more liberally than their critics. Definitions of sexual aggression have created a vexed issue that for understandable reasons began too narrowly with the premise of male senior and female subordinate; distinctions will be refined case by case, but as with other vexed issues, universal justice will not be obtained soon.

In John Silber's campaigns against tenure, he observed justly that tenure after probation as a safeguard of academic freedom left students, instructors, assistant professors, and most coaches without such guarantees. The U. S. Supreme Court held the views on qualification for tenure of this president of Boston University as fallible as the inelastic regent in Texas had found him, but Dr. Silber's observation that professors claim protection for errant opinions not encouraged among the untenured is correct and telling. With few exceptions, students enjoy, as the faculty does, academic freedom to learn. Academic freedom as an honor code increases the chances of freedom for student opinion; otherwise, protection of free speech outside the classroom will not assure justice in assessment of qualities. In law the distinction between adult and adolescent is an arbitrary line; in the slightly less arbitrary distinction between teachers and learners, the buck should stop with the teachers. But are older teachers immeasurably wiser than those younger? That tenure has become an obstruction to academic renewal, by maintaining apprenticeship but severely limiting advance into senior faculties, has created an opening for those arguing that procedures should be modified to include periodic review for elimination of the inadequately responsible and the incompetent.

Scrutiny and review need no defense; the problem is choice of judges. Who is to judge a given professor's competence? When incompetence is the word chosen to describe other than an opinion offensive to an influential member of the governing board, it usually identifies mediocrity, made an awkward criterion by the necessary presence of an average and a mean. Mediocrity can be identified; the average cannot be eliminated. Only faculty members speaking in private can be counted on to mean by the word *mediocre* genuine mediocrity.

The history of higher education in the United States demonstrates absolutely that only peers in a faculty can judge incompetence without malice arising from other grounds. And peers will not vote to dismiss without strong provocation. In the 1970s, seeking ways to retain for universities their best hope, by creating opportunity for superior assistant professors who would not otherwise be granted continuance under the barriers suddenly erected, I found that no university or college of the identifiable thirty-five that had instituted review, a few of them twenty or thirty years earlier, had achieved among them a single dismissal. According to George Will, who had a local informant, at the University of Texas in Austin, with 1,371 tenured professors in 1997, only 2 had been terminated in the last twenty-five years.

Two in thirteen hundred is about the same percentage as that of physicians publicly declared incompetent by other physicians. In four years the twenty thousand charges heard by the Civilian Complaint Review Board of New York City led to the dismissal of one police officer.[27] Walter Gellhorn explained in various lectures and articles that all requests for licensing to protect the public from malpractice and inferior performance have come from the groups to be licensed, with the strong implication that the purpose of the request is to restrict numbers and limit competition. Once inside the guild, however, membership is nearly sacrosanct. Institute review, then. Except for inefficient use of time, review is healthy; but nourish no exorbitant hope, unless your aim is to shred the intellectual fabric of higher education. Professors are not so unlike the rest of humanity that they will vote a colleague out of a position of employment when the power to close the position altogether lies elsewhere. For the managers of education, tenure is not a problem of quality but of budget. A teacher eliminated is a budget thereby reduced. Colleagues will not eagerly cast a vote that means they must absorb the chores of the dismissed. This threat has been a strong factor in the unionization of faculty in middle-range state universities. Such threats, along with management's progressive reduction in percentages of dedicated, experienced teachers, is forcing unionization as the only way to serve college students honorably in the future.

A survey in 1994 of review in two-year colleges and of 526 teachers at the University of Colorado and 618 at the University of Hawaii gave some indication that review of performance can encourage a few professors to retire when the criterion for successful performance is quantity of publication.[28] Otherwise, periodic review has so far been economically unprofitable. It has proved to be one more way to misuse faculty time.

Professors who cringe at the thought of dismissing the incompetent become less timid when considering dismissal of the irresponsible. Most professors have a strong sense of duty. If the absence of clear rules of conduct sometimes exposes a vague sense of direction in curiosity about where duty lies, an irresponsible colleague creates no divided loyalties. Honesty can be bent by temperament, and ennui invades all occupations, but among teachers of literature in North America, irresponsibility has been at least as rare as lunacy. The chance that earning a Ph.D. has not curbed temperament enough to subdue irresponsibility provides one of the reasons for the tenure system. During probation from teaching assistant through (sometimes) instructor to assistant professor (and often beyond), teachers learn the importance of believing themselves earnest. The flawless idea of cashiering the irresponsible will not solve the problems of budget.

A modification of tenure might improve the chances for intellectual strength in the twenty-first century. No other step into greater health, however, could equal instant reduction in the size of institutional bureauracies. College presidents before 1915 faced few hazards in terminating professors. Suspended between governing boards and administrative bureauracies, presidents now find it increasingly difficult to make decisions either innovative or routine. Since the 1930s presidents and chancellors have formulated and executed policies through an ever-mounting number of aides. No statistical precision is required to demonstrate that academic administrations have grown much faster than discoveries of new galaxies and black holes in the universe. Less than a century ago faculty and students performed almost all the duties of higher education except those of trustees or regents, president, secretary, dean, janitors, maids, a minimum of skilled workers, and, in a few universities, provost. Faculty determined admissions. The registrar, and in some universities the bursar, served from the faculty. One teacher was the librarian; other faculty members chose the books for purchase; students performed most of the chores to keep the library open. Administrative and departmental secretaries, for decades few in number, served for exploitative wages then as now. Unionization of maintenance personnel, library cataloguers, and other trained and untrained employees continued to be avoided well into the 1950s, on the plea that students needed part-time jobs as food-handlers, equipment managers in laboratories and gymnasiums, "stack rabbits" in the library, or similar operatives. In the 1930s fewer needy students than today were employed in such physical labor as upkeep of grounds, for manual labor seemed then an insignificant charge to the budget.

Concerned both for the intellectual progress of the nation and for the young PhDs who had toiled long for a diminished opportunity to think and to serve, and knowing that during the Great Depression the tenured faculty at the University of Wisconsin had voted for a 50 percent reduction in salary in order to retain on the faculty lecturers and instructors without tenure (when teachers in Chicago continued for a year without payment), I asked what had been done in those hard times at Columbia University.

To my astonishment, the payroll records of the university for the 1930s soon appeared on the desk before me. They made a stack less than one foot high. For each year members of the various faculties of the university were listed alphabetically by department. On each leaf in the left column the name of each faculty member; in the next column the annual salary; in the third column the amount of increase in annual salary recommended by the head of the department, $200, $100; in the final column, completed by the president, Nicholas Murray Butler, "100" or "50" or, most often, "No."

The files of that stack include also a letter from Butler asking the one assistant he utilized in running the university (a faculty member) to determine by personal canvass what the reaction would be if salaries were reduced by 10 percent in order to retain lecturers he would otherwise have to dismiss. (Under President Butler no teacher at Columbia had statutory tenure; apparently the reaction to Fackenthal's canvass was negative.) Even Harvard's Eliot and Lowell could have envied Butler, who ran his university from his telephone. Harvard after Lowell had the advantage of strong, commanding deans of Harvard College, while the infighting of internecine bureaucracies began to paralyze rival institutions.

Even with calculations and projections done by computer and lists regurgitated through word-processing, it would take ten administrators today just to carry from one office to another the amount of paper involved in comparative assessments for the purpose of determining salaries. At several Ivy League universities it has taken more administrators to recommend and achieve the closure of small departments than there were teachers and other employees in those disciplines.[29]

Colleges and universities advertise competitively their student-faculty ratios, but not their student-administrative ratios, nor, in major universities a comparison of student-faculty ratios in 1950 or 1960 with the ratios counting only full-time, continuing faculty at later dates. This is not to deny that ratios as a criterion of excellence also fail to say what the faculty was doing with the hours of an academic year but only to question the figures as evidence of expenditure for excellence. Universities could well boast of an enlarged contribution of academia to the gross national product. Individual students are showable but meager consumers in comparison with their managers.

In most of the annual financial reports, the lines and columns for "administrative" expense refer to the central administration; the various deans and their many subordinates in the arts and sciences, law, engineering, medicine, and the rest—including usually the separate institutes of research—are charged along with laboratories, departmental computers, and chalk as educational expense. Vincent Scully has been quoted as saying, "None of us who know Yale pay any attention to what they say about budgets."[30]

Hyder Rollins, Gurney Professor of English at Harvard, complaining of the phenomenal growth of executive officers in the 1950s, used to imitate the squeaky voice of Mrs. Moore, widow of *the* dean of Harvard College, when he would meet her in Harvard Square during the 1940s: "Oh, Mr. Rollins, do you remember when my husband and dear Mr. Lowell *ran* this university?—and just look at it now!"

Over time the burdens of administration borne by an Abbott Lawrence Lowell from 1909 to 1933 or a Nicholas Murray Butler from 1902 to 1945 were thought to be lightened by the addition of a vice president and occasionally an assistant dean. Next, two vice presidents, then three, then five, then a scattered seven, each with associates and assistants. In reports of the news media, the term *higher education* understandably includes the ever-growing, nonteaching administrations; usage often suggests that *higher* refers to administrators, with *teaching assistants* a term to distinguish teachers from other assistants. For each vice president, a staff; for each staff an increase in such supporting offices as payroll and maintenance. An institution with thirteen vice presidents may have an unlucky number. Financial difficulties in higher education come in part from excessive branching, as administrators declare, but they come also from progressive thickening of the stalk. The burden to teachers of service on committees seems much less a burden in those select institutions where decisions of a faculty committee define solutions rather than begin the worming of an issue through the bureauracy from which the issue came.

There has been an explosive growth into a million bachelor's degrees awarded annually in nearly four thousand institutions with a total faculty of nine hundred thousand.[31] Faced with phenomenal increase in numbers, university budgets nationally declined from 1982 to 1992 for libraries, for maintenance, and for instruction (even in the administrative arithmetic that counts deans' staffs as educational), but rose sharply for administration; in private universities administrative budgets increased 45 percent.[32] Between 1966–67 and 1991–92 in the University of California the number of students grew 97 percent, the instructional staff 61 percent, and the General Administration 151 percent; the expenditures for instruction rose by 175 percent, those for administration by 400 percent.[33] Some figures for other institutions appear below in the appendix.

From the 1940s to 1991 the percentage of research grants from Washington charged by universities for administering the grants increased with each increase in central administrations. By 1991 Stanford and Columbia were charging 74 percent of each grant to administrative costs, exceeded only by the Harvard Medical School at 79 percent; in October 1991 the White House Office of Management and Budget called a halt to escalation and set the maximum overhead on grants at 26 percent.[34]

Citing the *Digest of Education Statistics, 1993, 1994*; *Research in Higher Education, 1993*; and the *Chronicle of Higher Education Almanac, 1994, 1995* on the scene nationally, Lynn Hunt concludes:

> The size of the faculty has been increasing, by 30 percent between 1976 and 1989, when the number of students increased 25 percent, but the teaching environment has been subtly trans-

formed even for full-time, tenure-track faculty. . . . The number of administrators and nonteaching professionals employed by the university has increased most of all, by 43 percent for administrators and by 123 percent for "nonfaculty professionals" (many of whom we would probably consider administrators). The university staff as a whole is getting bigger, but the relative presence of faculty, secretaries, and janitors is actually declining. By 1991, the percentage of faculty within the total staff . . . had declined from 34 percent in 1976 to 32.5 percent . . . and the percentage of instruction and research assistants had declined from 8.6 percent to 7.8 percent, while the presence of nonfaculty professional staff had increased from 9.6 percent to 16.8 percent.[35]

There is some truth in administrative complaints that accounting to Washington for the way funds are used has required an increase in paper and in the shufflers of paper. (The office of Vice Provost for Educational Equity at Penn State includes twelve aids.) But the increase in reporting to Washington increases with the growing corpulence of administrations as much as with complexities of student life and is as nothing compared with the progressive increase required by administrative employees within the same university reporting to each other, often on data collected at the expense of faculty time that might have gone into the tasks of education. Martin Trow has insisted that presidents have not become mere mediators and can achieve autonomy through large administrative staffs—enabling them to put recalcitrant departments into receivership—but this analysis from personal experience significantly fails to mention the misinformation on which presidents currently act.[36]

Requirements by the national government account much less for the multitudes in administration than competitiveness and imitation. What Massachusetts does, Ohio will do. Stanford can expand its fields of study without expansion by Princeton, but what Stanford does administratively, Princeton copies. A professor of finance at the University of Chicago provided administrators with several reprintings, in the decade after 1944, of his book on saving dollars: "The ultimate objective of this volume is to increase the effectiveness of the business and financial management of colleges and universities."[37] Management increased; effectiveness did not.

University presidents are absolutely correct in declaring that university administrations today have to be large. But the reason that they have to be large is simply that they have become large, have become massive. An increase in the numbers of employees in the various financial offices requires an increase in the personnel office and in both the *personnel* and the *buildings* of buildings and grounds. A building for geology or astronomy requires an increase in endowment from donors, but a building or rented offices off campus for the central administration can be paid for out of general funds. It is easy enough to demonstrate to trustees that administrative activities, necessary as the university is currently organized, have outgrown the space and the facilities for methods of communication currently available. Ten or twelve or seventeen deans reveal educational complexity; offices of a central administration keep busy washing each other's linen. Employees numbering twenty thousand will consider themselves collectively vital to twenty-three hundred faculty and forty thousand students, but many of them are vital only to each other. Individually, most are poorly paid compared with persons in similar posts in corporations of mediocre earnings; only in the bulk do they drain educational resources; only their mass and their impercipient employers reduce the quality of higher education.

Donald Kennedy, as president emeritus of Stanford, continued to deny in 1993 any wrongdoing in charging 74 percent of research grants from the government as indirect reimbursement for general institutional costs and the costs incurred at the president's home, but what he had come to realize is worth quoting at length:

A particularly troublesome illustration of failed central planning in the past decade has been the management of institutional size and scope. At Stanford, as in other research universities, the 1980s saw significant growth in the size of staff compared with that of faculty or student body. Some of this was a response to increased transaction volume: more applications, more gifts to process, more regulatory requirements of all kinds. But the lion's share was "opportunistic growth" in areas not supported by the operating budget, like sponsored research. This growth in turn caused expansion of all the service elements of the institution: personnel, benefits, procurement, faculty/staff housing, and the like. As this infrastructure grew in complexity, two things became clear. First, it became less efficient, and service levels declined. Despite a high level of dedication on the part of individual staff members, faculty complaints about the quality of help they were getting increased even as the number of helpers was growing larger. Second, we began to recognize that the external costs of an enlarged staff rose in a nonlinear fashion—they were no longer met by the indirect cost revenues associated with the additional appointments.

These staff increases bear a major share of the responsibility for the "cost disease" that emerged for the universities in the 1980s. In a growth economy, such problems are masked. . . .

. . . We missed the vital linkage that coupled staff growth outside the primary academic budget to growth inside it, and we did not take preventive steps that might have saved the situation. In effect, we permitted restricted funds to tax the general fund. Nor did we perceive the revolution in personnel management that was beginning to take place in the profit sector—a revolution that might have allowed us to do more with less.[38]

Continuing increases in administration and administrative costs show that the problem was not merely sponsored research and that the lesson of downsizing for efficiency "in the profit sector" has not been effectively learned.

Analyze if you can the facts rather than the announcements of your alma mater to contrast the number of newly added classrooms in the last twenty years with the number of newly added offices, not forgetting additional administrative offices in spaces off the campus. New employees are hired, and office space for them found, to plan ways of shifting and combining the offices where departmental faculty hold conferences with students.

In announcing deficits for 1991 and 1992, Harvard administrators included the greatly increased costs of employee benefits. Since then the costs of health insurance have continued to rise. Benefits to the individual employee could be increased without escalating total costs if the number of employees for whom benefits are calculated were reduced. Commercial corporations began to learn at least twenty years ago that sweeping, extensive, wholesale reductions in middle management increase efficiency. Subsequent increases in some corporate managements reflect greater profitability in recent years but illustrate also the tendency of management to proliferate by bureaucratic replication. Higher education could be improved by reducing the numbers of secondary executives and their subordinates in the central administrations of colleges and universities; reduction of interactive middle management would not only improve efficiency but would also afford teachers more time for the purposes of education.

In a period when technological advances reduce in numbers the need for specialized as well as untrained employees, it brings no joy to recommend wholesale firings of competent individuals. My personal recommendation would be to transfer truckloads of administrators, with retraining where appropriate, into activities of direct benefit to the minds of students. Some of the best young teachers denied tenure have been accommodated in administration; it is time to move them back.

In 1971 college and graduate school enrollments remained high, but university administrators proclaimed foresight: by reducing the numbers of expensive senior faculty, they could forestall increased deficits from the expected drop in undergraduate admissions. Anticipation included also something more urgent than falling enrollments. Expansion in administrations and reduction in faculties came in part as protection against students. When violent protests against continuation of the war in Vietnam agitated academic institutions from coast to coast; when students were a formidable presence in the march of a quarter of a million people to Washington in November 1969, no action proposed seemed more promising than that mentioned earlier, reduction of contact between undergraduates and doctoral candidates serving as graduate assistants. Teaching assistants, however, are cheaper than experienced elders. Economic reasons joined political reasons for reducing the numbers and power of faculty at all levels. Teaching assistants, who themselves trusted nobody over thirty-five, were not only suspect; under the rules of tenure they were expendable wherever other part-time teachers could be found.

As past eras show, to have a university requires students, faculty, space for classes, library (and current telecommunications), equipment and supplies for laboratories, and an administrator. Without students and faculty, an institution would be something other than a university; much of everything else is self-serving. At least one columnist decrying the confiscatory increases in tuition has managed not to ignore the administrative center in identifying bloat: "Teaching Shakespeare to sophomores and buying books for the library are costs, of course. But so is giving a raise to the basketball coach, buying an espresso maker for the faculty dining room, hiring an assistant to the assistant affirmative-action director, paying monthly retainers to a high-powered lobbyist, building a new boathouse for the crew, or adding politically correct courses on 'Feminist Literature' and 'New Age Religions.' "[39] More recently there are also assistants to the assistant end-of-affirmative-action director. Not all news has cast gloom: the *Wall Street Journal* reported on September 30, 1997, that "the central personnel-services division" of the University of Southern California had recommended its own dissolution.

In a period of rapid transition from human workers to carefree electronics, it may be cruel to recommend terminations of employment even of such bugs in the machine as assistant vice presidents, but to call the present inefficiency in higher education wasteful is polite understatement. Management complains that it is the educational mission, the faculty, that diverts funds from successful management. As their mentor Peter F. Drucker advises in his books, in the Forbes magazines, and elsewhere, managers seek to quantify and control not merely costs but everything that might affect cost-accounting.

Journalists have deplored the high salaries of presidents, provosts, and coaches as if these were a chief cause of national deficits. The difficulty is that managers are being paid escalating salaries to reduce the quality of education. Employees who remain after a reduction for efficiency should receive a living wage, which many have not received. Meanwhile, concentration on a few salaries is to notice the wildebeests while ignoring the swarms of mosquitoes that outweigh an elephant. Confining arrogance to the highest levels of administration would considerably improve higher education. What is at stake is not the future of universities but the future of education.

CHAPTER SIX

Now and Tomorrow

Where does literary study go from here? Many roads are possible, none paved with gold, but one or two can be made viable by good will. As the most urgent problems in education and society fester below the college level, in the dysfunctional relationships of parent and education, in reading, writing, arithmetic, inertia, and crime, it would be treasonable of the clerks in higher education to avoid attendance on those problems. Universities can best attend to their own business by directing energies toward the socialization of the adolescent population, with attention also to what the French call *l'enfance*, which passes at age twelve into the cumulative problems of *l'adolescence*.

The present plea comes from one culpably ignorant of primary education and of details in the attention higher education will need give to barriers erected against optimum results, but custodians of literature in higher education have an interest, at the very least, in having children learn to read with pleasure instead of coercing them into reading "as early as possible, as much as possible, and even as fast as possible."[1] If children in the lowest grades learn to read with pleasure, microprocessing firms can do limited damage in wanting them trained in later grades as future employees.

For a later stage, when literary study will be a minor concern of the healthy teenager, the temporary and the durable accomplishments of the Civilian Conservation Corps (CCC) of 1933–42 bring a strong conviction that no other segment of the social remedies needed today could serve as many commendable purposes as conscription of every able youth, for two years or nigh about, with choice of national conservation, local community service, or a military stint. Ideally, a few could be selected on merit for mentoring younger children. Nations of sterner management than the United States might begin such service in the transition from *l'enfance* or soon after, but the inevitably political inclusion of military service presupposes a period between school and college or adult job.

Service in national or community conservation need not follow as closely as the CCC did the patterns of military command. The inclusion of local community service, besides weakening several objections to required enlistment, would give greater reality to the buzzword *community*. Many painters, printmakers, sculptors, and writers were permanently grateful for the Work Projects Administration (WPA) (and muralists and sculptors also for the Federal Administration of Public Works [PWA]), and others should have been permanently grateful, because the New Deal, when the need was economic, preserved artists as well as works of art and knowledge of the past. The WPA provided both independence and a sense of purposeful fellowship. When the need is social—from crimes against the haves and crimes against the have-nots—a shared supplementary education would be a national boon. We have to imagine first, of course, at least one elected representative of conscience and vision.

Before the end of World War II, naval ships were equipped with packets of the Hutchins-Adler Great Books to promulgate issues of the war; students of literature, when the need is both economic and moral, could readily identify less combative authors to include along with Hobbes and Wollstonecraft for conveying issues of peace. Assuming failure in the national will to solve problems declared deplorable by nearly everybody, faculties on their own ground in colleges and universities might beneficially promote "experiental education," assignments that send students out to make Balzacian studies of human behavior, with academic brownie points for community service.[2]

Nearest to home, senior colleges and universities need to form reciprocal alliances with secondary schools and community colleges. Reciprocity is the only way with hope for improvement. Alliance should also include the preparation of graduate students for teaching in community colleges and secondary schools—in ways that would be welcomed by those institutions. There was a time when college departments of English, foreign languages, mathematics, and classics should have worked closely with public schools to determine the content of specific courses. Instead, they used a pocket weapon still available: specification by fiat or examination of requirements for admission into college. When employed, that weapon is effective in mathematics for that portion of the young continuing into college. For literacy, the problem begins at the age when a child should be able to read and intensifies soon after when the child should be encouraged to hand-hold a book. For English teachers, greater problems than literary content need cooperative action. E. D. Hirsch Jr. has no doubt performed a service to more than the Core Knowledge Foundation in collaborating on a guide for parents and teachers that lists books purveying the cultural literacy he recommends.[3] Exactly what belletristic works high schools should assign, however, is not a question that most college teachers have prepared themselves to answer intelligently.

To make the discussion comfortable, let's assume that secondary and college teachers of English agree on the aims of helping students to speak and write the American language with clarity and vigor and to recognize, and at least minimally to analyze, subtlety of thought, feeling, and expression in works selected for strength in expression, feeling, or thought. How to achieve these aims can best be determined by teachers of reading and writing at all levels consulting and arguing as equals.

In proposing cooperation among levels of education, we must also consider the college teacher of English, French, or German (more likely than the teacher of Spanish or Norwegian) who believes that life is semiotic, that the human mind can know experience only as representation, that a work of literature can have significance but no determinable meaning, that halos should be removed from Homer, Dante, Shakespeare, Goethe, Tolstoy, and the illusion of creativity. Theory pursuing these avenues has produced discourse on what literature cannot be and cannot do. If literature can never be more than an analyzable game, every professor of literature has a moral duty to know it. Certainly no course in the history of criticism should halt before reaching this question.

If such indeterminacy were granted, what is the earliest age appropriate for learning that poetry makes nothing happen, that a poem can be but cannot mean, that works of drama and fiction are representations drawing not upon reality but upon representational language, that language can have known only its one hypothetical creator, Adam, and that reading not professionally informed is not reading at all? How long after learning that all those red-suited guys in the malls can't be Santa Claus should a child know that language, not Whitman, wrote "O Captain! My Captain!"? Can we catch the child early enough, joining in a timely way the marriage of television and the world wide web, to instill a lasting conviction of the inutility of literature? If we can, before this fad passes, hundreds of courses in Renaissance, Romantic, and postmodern literature will be freed of students, and professional training can be classified as theory adumbrated in French, theory adapted to American tastes, and theory claiming an origin in languages other than French, German, or Italian.

The point of this exaggeration is to observe that strict theory has remained within professional boundaries, except when books on the subject have been publicly reviewed. Only professors who teach courses designated as criticism or literary theory have carried rigidity of method very far into undergraduate classrooms. Most college teachers of English are neither one-eyed nor binocular, but bifocal or cross-eyed. What they advocate in learned journals, except for the avoidance of such antique concerns as intention and manifest context, is not what they practice in a survey of literature for sophomores. But some of the thought given to professional exchange ought to be given to the guidance of transitions in reading from childhood to college. Can professors say to teachers of English in secondary schools something other than "No author has ever come down a chimney" or the more customary "Who are you to ask?"?

If professional students of literature wish the power of recruiting disciples, they should begin to aid—should devote time to aiding—secondary teachers in encouraging children to read well-contrived works of narrative and items of patterned language for pleasure and self-discovery. Those in English departments torn between professionalization-beyond-hermeneutics and affection for traditional methods of interpretation could profitably direct their affective impulses toward the more heavily massed problems of teachers domesticating grades four through twelve. Considering that 40 percent of higher education occurs in community colleges, university professors might give serious attention to the National Council of Teachers of English. For those of divided impulse, intellectual ingenuity can be exercised with dignity in seminars for apprentice prelates; nostalgia for the thrill of encountering "The Secret Sharer" or Emily Brontë's "Remembrance" or Marianne Moore's "Poetry" for the first time can be shared in colloquy with teachers whose textbooks contain those successors to Longfellow, Whittier, and Holmes that seem so unspeakable to the professor who writes on Borges and Barthelme. One until now ashamed to bathe in the Schopenhauerian stream of Macleish's "You, Andrew Marvell" could take vicarious pleasure from contemplating high school students successfully challenged to discover the palpable devices of that poem. A professor accustomed to unraveling the intricacies of Wallace Stevens and Geoffrey Hill could without humiliation read simpler, rollicking verse aloud with fervor to third-graders. And could meet effective teachers in the process.

Professors of literature have believed themselves lax for not taking time to say to children in the public schools what superior knowledge enables them to say to English majors in college. One who holds or has embarked upon study for a Ph.D. in English or American literature has not been trained to teach the illiterate to read, but the teaching of English as a second language is near at hand in most universities, and methods of demonstrable success in teaching illiterates, young and old, can be learned even by English majors. The necessary patience will be harder to acquire.

In most ways cooperation between preparatory and college teachers should be more extracurricular than curricular; that is, college needs to be different from high school and there is no harm in high school being different from college. Before 1945 a college teacher did not call a student by the first name; employing *Mr.* and *Miss* enforced the idea that college accommodated only adults and differed in method and intellectual stringency from any previous education. Since then, able students have often protested that introductory courses required in the freshman year boringly repeat what had been learned in preparatory programs. Both views are symptoms of the failure of communication between colleges and earlier stages of education.

Something can be said for the proposition that the usual progression from the broadest generalizations in courses for beginners in college through narrower and narrower focus along the way to a dissertation on the imperceptible should be reversed, that freshmen should be taught methods of research by concentration sharp enough to prompt independent exploration and mastery. At the top of a widening gyre, in this inversion of conventional procedure, a doctoral dissertation would demonstrate some aspect of the proposition that Aristotle, Sophocles, Aquinas, and Pascal looked too narrowly at human problems.

When we ask a different question in a larger context, what the university of the twenty-first century should be doing, the answer takes us from a concentration on youth to consideration of a population aging into and beyond maturity. Adults are not waiting for their seventies to seem as directionless as they believe their own and everybody else's grandchildren to be. Adult education is the kind of education colleges should begin to take seriously. That is, college education, as distinguished from the old college spirit, should be adult, should think adult.

Allan Bloom was almost 180 degrees off in declaring that "colleges do not have enough to teach their students, not enough to justify keeping them four years, probably not even three years."[4] Colleges have so many treasure chests no one unfamiliar with the arranged choices in folklore can guess which is best to open. Systemless electives nevertheless inspire thoughts of a three-year program for youth. Early in the twentieth century the spread of Harvard's elective system made Johns Hopkins, Yale, and Chicago contemplate three years for the B.A., and the professional schools at Columbia convinced President Butler that two years would suffice.[5]

In the 1970s college presidents emerged from conclaves in agreement that the four-year degree should give way to three years after high school and then, after a lapse into maturity, a return for a fourth year of directed education. They spoke feelingly of the great need of adults for enlightenment and refreshment through continuing education. It turned out, however, that presidents (whose average term of office was then three years) were focused entirely on disruptions. As soon as the demonstrations and student occupation of buildings declined, the improvement of mature minds, made ready for college by experience, lost significance. In most universities, adult, continuing education became frivolous decoration unattached to serious curricula. Petty cash could be earned by teaching adults defensive driving, basket-weaving, finger-painting, and moving a computer mouse or joystick for interactive games.

Intellectual refreshment for adults, at more or less specified intervals, is an opportunity and a need. The educational system of eleven or twelve years plus four was devised when an individual life had fewer segments than the health sciences and health industries make possible today. A teenager frets under the necessity of choosing a major; an adult can choose a new career or choose to enrich a career begun years ago in inadequacy. Most teachers can recognize in the performance of older students evidence that continuation from high school, with its hazing and four-year athletic competitiveness, is a muddy ditch compared to the alluvial deposit of platinum that is potential in the continuing education of adults. With serious, systematized adult education, colleges could reduce their investment as residential resorts. Thought would then probably have to be given, and could be, to new ways of paying for athletic equipment. Returning adults will not greatly increase the parking problems. Serious continuing education for adults, however, will require not only an increased number of evening classes but also an initially astute manipulation of staff. Classes scheduled for employed adults would mitigate slightly the present embarrassment of well-equipped classrooms and lecture halls occupied for little more than 9 A.M. to 5 P.M., Monday through Thursday and on to Friday noon, for what amounts, on the semester system, to nine months of the year. If college teachers are professionally active fifty-odd hours a week, most college classrooms certainly are not. Idle rooms and equipment make students seem badly distributed nationally, like office workers living in a suburb and driving through the city to work in a rural edifice on the other side. Universities need adults; adults need the refreshment and strength of education.

How can we adapt for a genuine system of lifelong education what has grown like toadstools for a four-year cycle, "library, stadium, student unions, commons or dining halls, co-op housing, off-campus fraternity and sorority houses, Quonset huts" and the adjacent "restaurants, bookstores, coffeehouses, and bars"?[6] Chance has provided a usable vista. Feminist and ethnic studies have taken a step toward the university focused on problems, a future that could draw on chaos theory to reach "the synthetic, top-down big picture, meaning-making thought that is part of mature adult learning," cross-disciplinary and cross-cultural.[7] This quoted way of describing it shows that English teachers have a role to play in getting us from murkiness to clarity, but does not negate the viability of a focus on problems.

A house or college system, as at Yale, Harvard, Princeton, Rice, and other institutions that have given thought to undergraduates, will provide a special incentive for preserving the focus on fresh arrivals from high school; wherever reforms continue in the effort to achieve coherence in a college, all undergraduate courses and curricula should ideally be removed from departments and supervised by divisional or collegewide committees. Such merging of disciplines presupposes the continuation of colleges for the young, but it erects no barrier to the reeducation or refreshment of adults. Planned collegially, the fourth curricular year would be designed for returning adults.

Those entranced by visual culture and convinced that the book has no future will ask how the age of students tomorrow can be a concern of literary study. A quarter of a century ago New York University reported to a supportive foundation success at doubling the number of students taught in a single class of freshman composition. Twenty students sat in a room with the instructor and twenty more in a room with a television screen. The instructor, employing "the Socratic method," anticipated and answered such questions as the students in the second room might be thinking of. An assistant professor of computer sciences at DePauw University invents an electronic blackboard to eliminate inefficient note-taking by a laser device that transmits the writing on the board to computer terminals on each desk.[8] With less difficulty, a personal camcorder can capture what is said and how it is said as well as what is written or drawn. Personal camcorders in the classroom a university can ban as unfair dissemination, but commercial rivals will fight back. The threat of superior competitors may make enterprising universities think again about systemless electives.

In 1990 the Teaching Company of Springfield, Virginia, entered a field then very small with audio and video versions of professors lecturing in the classroom. A CD-ROM can add to the recorded lecturer visual and auditory materials available in the classroom only with competing electronic equipment. With the device invented at DePauw, each student can edit and insert personal comments—a feature still one step away for most instructional CD-ROMs and digital video discs. Meanwhile, the hypermedia provide hypertexts, contextual paths leading

outward from a painting by D. G. Rossetti, a manuscript, a first printing, a final version, and a virgin or two other than Rossetti's "Blessed
Damozel" at the center—but omit from an informatively "interactive"
offer to provide links into other contexts anything like critical contem-
plation.[9] Hypertexts, which offer endless possibilities to researchers,
offer to the great potential audience for literature a diversion from the
main road. To consider what you have seen in a rapid video manipulation is not the same as reflection in the presence of Michelangelo's
Moses. It may be that students released into the internet and into interactive video networks can, by seeking links to multiple contexts of
information, achieve collaborative learning.[10] It may also be that the
price will be a high charge against mission for traditional institutions to
compete in an industry that grows by upgrading; in a careful and
informed assessment, linking information technology strategically to
mission is declared "an unmet challenge."[11] Computer art differs in
usable ways from lithography, and will have to be taught because it
exists, but it is not an advance in the arts to match the gains digital
imaging has brought to medical practice. The increasing numbers
arriving in colleges each year do not come because today-conscious
administrators provide in classrooms today's (soon yesterday's) electronic equipment. Universities need to keep in view specific purpose,
general mission, and tomorrow. Make no mistake, the effect of digital-
ization on literature and literary study will be, not merely profound but
the greatest in the history of alphabets. The question is whether those
effects can be controlled or directed by humanists. Irreversible destruction of materials from four centuries of print culture began with the
advent of inaccurate reproduction on microfilm. The immediate local
concerns will be the escalating costs of maintaining access to knowledge
and expression through progressively modified and newly perishable
media.

Many professors of literature now look toward classrooms with dig-
itally fed screens on which all the world's libraries and all the world's
art will be interactively available in sharply pictorial, digital-surround

multimedia. Erica Jong virtually reads "The Buddha in the Womb" for the class while behind her a fetus, superimposed on a Buddha inhaling Oms, curls semiotically toward the picture in a picture, which transmits to each student's terminal a bibliography of Jong studies, with certified quotations. A modem is the ultimate multicultural machine.

If that is what lies a few years ahead, cannot universities then mired in obsolescence of equipment get along without those departments that have the *least* need for specimens, equipment, or experiments? If volumes that fit the hand cease to be the basis of literary study, volumes like the Library of America that can be taken to bed; if ironies of the narrative voice in *Gulliver's Travels*, *Northanger Abbey*, and *The History of Henry Esmond* need no face-to-face tutorial guidance; if Lizzie Borden cannot discuss with a live adviser the trouble she is having with her parents; then there may be a blob with twelve or twenty fingers at the door. Universities succumbing to new technologies may need researchers but will they employ teachers? They will need teachers; the experience of those who have employed word processors in the teaching of introductory composition reveals the limitations of self-instruction at a distance from the truly interactive teacher; but managers would prefer to believe in the processor. Does the escalating destruction of irreplaceable bound volumes that has come from overconfidence in the durability of electronic records foreshadow a downsizing of more than libraries? The economic threat is a Godzilla: what would it take to secure electronic educational marvels as the talking point of universities if competitors can offer a discount? No sane person has claimed that words are more readable on a computer screen than in a well-printed book; the progression has been from woodblock to photograph to color to movement to computer manipulation.

Of course professors of literature should feel free to employ all the technological toys available. Always, however, teachers of language and literature, particularly, need to bear in mind that the picture worth a thousand words can provide no clear picture of the word "worth" in that phrase. The only successful competitor against words for conveying value is money. In an era reportedly visual, English teachers could be cheered by the large role television gives to faces talking—often when the talk is not notable for rhetorical skills or logic. Equipment more interactive than television can heighten a student's interest in, say, composition, but it will not reduce the preparation, directing, and correcting time of a conscientious teacher.

For advanced classes and even in introductory courses, the sirens calling to departments of language and literature, including English, have not been ethnic cultures so much as visual arts. Literature and painting have been called sister arts immemorially, and much in literature and literary history can be illustrated visually in the classroom, but specific comparisons can be made more appropriately in presentations at conferences and in illustrated books than in a course by one trained only in literature and language who attempts to give equal weight to verbal and visual effects. No lecturer can be more accurate in describing a painting than in showing a representation of it; what I would warn against, for most of us, is "equal weight."

Courses that compare film versions with novels or dramas that served in preparing the scenario have the advantage for comparison of narrative extended through time. Such courses can throw strong light on the differing techniques of fiction, stage, and cinema. Even if the teacher has no other motive than belief that students enter saturated in movies and television, appreciation and comprehension of literary works can be heightened by attention to dissimilar techniques. Musicological courses in opera gain demonstrably from contrasts of libretto and opera with pictorial, fictional, and dramatic versions of subject or icon.

As every student will arrive versed in interactive visual games from CD-ROM and the internet or the successors of DVD-ROMs and such, ancillary tools of visual interaction can be expected in these courses as in every other, from nanoscience to medieval balladry. The multicultural teacher will feel free to ask students to employ E-mail for contact not only with differing cultures but with what might be called levels of culture on the Interstreet.[12] It would be at least as valuable to have students make an experimental laboratory of real streets. Technology removes information at increasing distances from wisdom. When one assumes that professors of Spanish, French, or German bring no moral presence to the classroom, then a keyboard and monitor become the ideal for basic training in a language, natural as well as mathematic. Teachers of language and composition can certainly heighten interest within the disinclined by utilizing processors and visual enhancement.

Arthur Levine of Teachers College, Columbia University, expects interactive electronic education by "distance learning," each individual before a keyboard and monitor, to reduce the number of campuses needed in state systems of higher education.[13] Levine recognizes the related threat to universities from entrepreneural competition, and in the same number of *Daedalus* Walter E. Massey notes the increase in private educational institutions established by corporations with technological savvy.[14] These trends can be expected to accelerate as the technology for distance learning improves. The introduction of electronics on campuses has usually brought employment to more persons, not fewer, but management has not chosen to accompany an increase in technology with an increase in teachers.

A much larger question than teachers of literature can answer is being asked globally: Why should parents or other adults pay the administrative and maintenance costs of buildings used four and a half days a week, seven hours a day at most, for a service that entrepreneurial firms can perform at a much lower cost and probably better? The entrepreneurs have available all the devices they need to supplant courses in visual culture. Such profitable institutions as the University of Phoenix, with forty thousand students in 1997 and totally without an edifice complex, will have a more dedicated access than traditional colleges to the decorated information of the near future. Anyone who has watched the inefficiency introduced into the registration process by the purchase of computers and computer operators knows that technology does not show its best face in traditional colleges. Financial officers of universities in the Ivy League and near San Francisco will answer, in private, that they do not charge for education but for degrees, for prestige. Entrepreneurs already answer that they can buy the use of the best minds, can buy names prestigiously elevated by elite universities and learned societies, can replace institutions with superstars who love to slamdunk.

Cyberspace has the potential commercially to make the virtual classroom the one with clientele and patrons. Paul Woodring, noting that the choice of four years for college "is little more than a historical accident," observed wryly that sitting in class persisted because "no one has yet found a better way of teaching large masses of students."[15] His "yet" was 1968. Peter F. Drucker, acknowledged master of management, predicts:

> Thirty years from now the big university campuses will be relics. Universities won't survive. It's as large a change as when we first got the printed book. . . .
>
> Such totally uncontrollable expenditures, without any visible improvement in either the content or the quality of education, means that the system is rapidly becoming untenable. Higher education is in deep crisis. . . .
>
> Already we are beginning to deliver more lectures and classes off campus via satellite or two-way video at a fraction of the cost. The college won't survive as a residential institution. Today's buildings are hopelessly unsuited and totally un-needed.[16]

If competition from entrepreneurs is not yet a serious threat, the reason lies in the inferiority of the virtual to a community of competent individuals. A personal computer with a modem can reduce the need to travel for research. Computers have increased precision in editing and have greatly improved analyses of style, content, and authorship. A classroom computer is an immense aid in teaching its own kinds of search. So far, the computer has been in the humanities a transcendent typewriter, an innovative research tool, and a teaching toy. Interactive communication among students on computers in one room or many is an admittedly attractive version of underinstructed chaos.

One version of the future foresees a student selecting from cyberspace one "best" course from each outstanding institution: mathematics from M.I.T. or Cal Tech, Spanish from Stanford or Texas, world literature from Brown. Video replaces the lecturer, but live bodies conduct sections and conferences. Without exclusive use of an elite faculty, the Ivies could still boast of offering undergraduates the opportunity to rub elbows with fellow students destined to be tomorrow's employers and chieftains. Boasts of elite faculty and students may then be reduced to reliance on students from families of influence. Meanwhile, institutions short on applicants destined by family for leadership seek to accumulate Merit Scholars. Already, the fastest growing segment of administration in small colleges and universities is the admissions office, now devoted to recruiting. Enrollment in community colleges, with the freedom to pick up part-time teachers at will, is increasing at almost four times the rate in four-year colleges. Commercial competition, if clever enough, could increase the efforts of college recruiting substantially. In North America, the open university could be opened widest by entrepreneurs.

In the minds of some, universities have themselves encroached by introducing remedial courses for students not ready for college. Critics of a conservative bent have protested that universities should leave remedial education to community colleges; but if universities continue with the same attitude toward entrepreneurial educators they have long maintained toward public schools, applicants for admission who have previously been intellectually deprived may become a welcome source of income for "elite" universities. Traditional colleges have begun to compete desperately with community colleges in advertising courses and programs that teach skills. The moral question is not whether older institutions lose dignity by programs in remedial reading, but whether they are equipped and committed to perform this task as well as community colleges are.

The teacher in today's urban public schools, modern equivalent of the Victorian maiden presiding over a one-room schoolhouse, trying to get everybody out alive at the end of each day, may not have accomplished much else. In the college classroom, persons fresh from defending their first book, the dissertation, are not prepared to confront the survivors from unsuccessful schooling; they have not been fitted by their professors to believe that teaching the uneducated to read is an honorable task. What the senior professor of literature was doing has seemed highly desirable and gratifyingly easy. Why stoop to a tougher job than selling Donne and Keats to English majors? For remedial education, motivation is paramount for both teacher and pupil. In remedial education, questions of talent and ability must take second place to questions and answers concerning the student's motivation. In distinctly limited experience, I have watched aspirants in courses of remedial writing (i.e., remedial reading) undergo repeated humiliation from inability to understand simple sentences—persevering because they wanted permission to take a second course required for a certificate in nursing or culinary arts. Two of the most honorable students I sponsored in New York City declined to complete their dissertations when forced to discover enormous satisfactions from lifting earnest illiterates into a full first year at a community college.

Do all they can, high school teachers will send out of their classrooms, along with the highly talented and committed, pupils resistant to tutelage. (Some of the world's greatest writers have been resistant at that stage.) Weekly columnists who believe they were ennobled by courses in Shakespeare, Milton, and trigonometry spray moral scorn on the adoption of remedial courses in English and mathematics by traditional colleges. They are willing to condone two-year colleges dedicated in part to forklifting inadequate recipients of high school diplomas into the semblance of novices in higher education, but find four-year colleges demeaned by attention to supplicants with an SAT less than fourteen hundred.

Moral scorn may have a just basis in the financial impetus behind remedial courses for prefreshmen in universities, but judgment should be directed instead toward degree of success. Within a university, the author of a dissertation on subtext in Molière or the hypocrisy of a tribute to the manor house brings little enthusiasm to the effacement of illiteracy on the diminutive scale of remedial workshops. Yet graduate assistants in English have been in universities the only persons allowed to perform the task with honor; almost anybody else undertaking the feat of attacking illiteracy within a university is a disrespected person performing a disreputable chore. Wherever a lack of enthusiasm fails to eliminate cases of success, let remedial work respectfully proceed. Honor the community college that has feared to employ teachers who have even contemplated the writing of a doctoral dissertation; honor also the college that has instead sought young teachers inspired by the hope of reducing illiteracy and fired by success in helping previously halted individuals to cope.

Another course taught as often as remedial English by the unready is English as a second language. Even in colleges of the United States with no students needing remediation, a program of English as a second language is needed, particularly in institutions with an international appeal, and a considerable number of teachers have to learn how to teach English as a second language. This challenge can be met. Courses specifically in teaching a second language to an adult or near adult rest so completely on theory that such training, in any event, cannot equal in significance thorough knowledge by the teacher of the students' native languages. Whether the teacher's field is English or another, it takes intimacy with the student's native culture to predict what will be done with American English learned in a course. Interactive processors may well prove superior to the average teacher in this task of improving the ability of immigrants and the children of immigrants to cope with the primary language in their place of residence.

The nation could well regard the problem of students coming to college with command only of a foreign language as minor compared with the problem of students coming to college, and leaving, with competence in no foreign language. Digital translation is possible, but not yet generally practical, and as someone said of IBM's Big Blue chess champion, if you tell the machine 2 x 2 = 78 it will believe you. The value of a foreign language doubles in an agile mind.

Like the noisy opposition to bilingual classes for Hispanic children, stridency against ethnic studies may further erode the small mound of foreign languages now possessed by the population of the United States. Regarding foreign and native languages, several foundational axioms can be declared: (1) The higher the percentage of residents with a working command of English, the more peaceful and productive the future of the United States will be. (2) In a global economy, the command of languages other than English is an asset to any adult American. (3) Bilingual children should be encouraged to master both languages and to study the literatures of both. (4) If students read works in translation, learning is improved by having a teacher who knows the original language. (5) Reading skilled stylists in the original language is a multiplied pleasure.

As one corollary of these axioms, colleges and universities should continue to require competence in at least one language excluding English and any language native to the student. One important purpose of the foreign language requirement is lost if a native language is allowed to satisfy the requirement. Two years of French may not lead to mastery of Gallic culture, but it will convey much more than vocabulary and grammar. It follows also from the axioms that professors of language and literature should plan, and their (more numerous) students should execute, methods of teaching English to children for whom it will be a second language or a first to be comprehended. We have few enough citizens bilingual in the speech of Maine and of South Carolina. (As it is far too late to require legally that the language must be English in a nation that speaks varieties of American—Oscar Wilde declared England and America divided by a common language—the word *English* in this discussion means American English, a term that fortunately can accommodate Canadian English.)

Reductions in the requirement of languages come in part from deceptive beliefs that translations adequately convey the nuances of literature and those of commercial transactions and that the global use of English makes all the world pleased hearers of the American voice, but most of all from avoiding what children regard as difficult or onerous. Rousseau has been misunderstood as recommending that the teacher choose what pleases the child. Rather, he commended methods of teaching that would engage the interest of the child in what needs to be taught, the advantage of making the child learn through pleasure from a sense of choice. Rousseau recommends against blocking the child's view by standing in front when you can more effectively push from behind. No child, and a minority among adults, prefers improvement to entertainment.

When improvement is the issue, remedial writing (or remedial reading), English for the unenglished, meets advanced courses on a level field. The teacher in a community college that mitigates illiteracy has improved citizenship in the nation. Mitigation is an honorable aim, almost as praiseworthy as improvement.

Nothing has made me more thoughtful about literary study than the prefatory remarks in a course guide prepared by and for students of Columbia and Barnard Colleges in the early 1960s. The remarks began by declaring the departments of English the best departments in the two colleges. The remarks continued by describing the skill of those English teachers in distinguishing infallibly among compositions meriting D, C, B, or A. The remarks concluded by declaring that students whose writing deserved C got C; those deserving A got A; it was not clear that any English teacher ever improved anybody's writing, but they could recognize good and bad writing when they saw it.

For me the kind of review attributed to deathbed reverie became instant revelation. Most of us as college teachers of literature had been assigning A's to the bluebooks of students sensitive to literary values if they were also skilled in conveying their reactions in language both accurate and expressive. We explained on the bluebooks of less literary students what they were missing. We could scold superior students for careless error, we could discover among them some who had not identified by name dramatic irony, eclogue, or litotes, but we could almost never be sure that we had made any student a more sensitive reader. We led them to intricate works they might not otherwise have read, and the language of close reading and available theories provided ways of asserting professionalized distinctions, but the task of permanently improving each student's style, not just the expression in a particular piece of writing but the logic and momentum of writers with or without promise, and the task of deepening each reader's taste and sensibility, form higher challenges that the English teacher should feel obligated to meet. It is not enough to recognize the presence or absence of informed choice, uncluttered reasoning, vocabulary accumulated from careful reading, and forceful clarity of expression; the English teacher should do the harder work of improving these.

Most college teachers of the requisite introductory composition confront students less than desperately motivated. Even if the student has not been prepared by an older brother or sister to dislike this course, a neighbor or personal experience with English teachers will have effectively lowered expectations. Teachers of other courses right off, and larger circles later, crave from this labor-intensive course in logic and rhetoric positive evidence of clarity in speech and writing. Positive results require weekly correction, and could profitably employ daily correction, of compositions unlikely to be ideally arranged into paragraphs that demonstrate or persuade by vigorous expression of organized thought. The desired result will seldom be obtained if a section meeting three or four times a week has more than twenty students writing weekly and will not be obtained consistently if any one teacher marks the papers from more than two such sections. Although the use of word processors may not erect new barriers, it will not obviate these.

Who is to perform this repetitive task? In a small college of liberal arts most teachers in the humanities and social studies can be persuaded by a well-composed directive to correct weekly writing if a common course includes content of sufficient range. Eliminating the shared course and instead having every teacher of an introductory course within a range of departments mark compositional errors and weaknesses in required weekly writing has led a few deans here and there to ignore the chaotic failure that ensues.

A large university up to its scalp in matriculations will have done the arithmetic long since: enlarge the graduate program in English sufficiently to ensure a pool of teaching assistants paid a pittance beyond exemption from tuition; provide the teaching assistants with a supervisor from the faculty, temperament of an archangel, to ensure effective methods of teaching. Parents and newspaper columnists who ignore the arithmetic implore trustees or regents to squash this frugal system and require senior professors to substitute for hours of research attention to the writing of tender novices. Figures exaggerated in favor of this proposition would be ten senior professors in English, one thousand entering students, or fifty senior professors, five thousand entering students, in institutions of either size disserving one hundred students in each section, or, with sections of twenty, one-fifth of the students having writing marked by senior faculty, with parents of the other four-fifths complaining bitterly.

Their complaints would be almost certainly without justification. At various times professors at Dartmouth and Amherst have insisted that marking the compositions of the alert students selected for admission to their care is a lifelong pleasure. Perhaps professors elsewhere should never have been allowed to regard the correction of freshman grammar and punctuation as an apprenticeship they have overcome through attention to Chaucer or Melville. This historic accident aside, few senior professors make effective tutors. The sop to parents and columnists at Harvard and elsewhere, having exceptional senior professors lecture to three hundred or more freshmen, has little direct effect on ability to write well. In the 1760s all Harvard tutors taught rhetoric, elocution, and English composition.[17] They did it because they were not professors. The one person in a large university who absolutely does not want full professors teaching composition to beginners is the person charged with supervising the methodology of the course.

As for the optimum size of a class, forget the fantasy that this country will choose to afford it. Writing should be guided by one-to-one tutorial, like a publisher's reader shaping a best-seller. It was Arthur Guiterman who transferred Mark Hopkins from a bench to a log, but in the great schools of England a fulcrum produced effective writers from repeated rewriting under the unforgiving eye of an individual tutor: the tutor sinks, the pupil rises and leaps. Failing perfection, twelve in a class would be better than the workable number of twenty.

Elders now lamenting the decline in public education voted criminally, at midcentury and later, to underfund public schools. Why can't Johnny read? One identifiable reason, among many more general faults in the society, is that English teachers in public schools, in what are now regarded as better days, were assigned no fewer than thirty pupils in each of two or more sections with a recommended theme or written report on the week's reading assignment each Friday—because Friday allowed no complaint about needing a day for correcting these sixty or more themes. These teachers had "home rooms," served as librarian and debating coach, and frequently had some such chore as coach of a squad giving moral support to the boys' athletic teams. The job of producing clear writers could positively not be done.

As themes overflowing the bedroom could not be intelligently marked in the time available, one alternative was borrowed from progressive schools. Instead of vain attempts to correct that mass of illegible scribbling, a core program could diffuse the class's attention. Play a contemporary sonata on a tape machine. Have three talented pupils draw on the blackboard what the music reminds them of. Then ask each pupil to write on a sheet of tablet paper what they think of the visual responses to the music. Have each pupil exchange with a neighbor the written response to drawings made in reaction to the sonata. Choose two or three strong readers and one or two weak readers to recite aloud the words before them. Complete this escalating acculturation with general discussion. The teacher grades the result after glancing at each paper, impossibility overcome. The consequent sense of doing something set the teacher on the path toward those in New York City whose one aim was to avoid murderous confrontations. In a period of still greater stress the English teacher will greet with smiles the supersession of tedious marking of errors by colorful computer games. Overtaxed like most, public school teachers of English are also overtasked. Complaints about foolish methods in the public schools neglect to observe that teachers unable to civilize what parents have made barbaric are escaping from overtaskation into sanity. Higher education, in succession to K–12, inherits the damage parents and other voters—including professors—have created by truancy.

If we follow the student of English in training to be a college teacher, we begin with graduate study and go next to the teaching of freshman composition. What should graduate study of literature be like? The perdurable *P*'s (Ph.D. as union card, publishing for promotion, and periodization) have a hammerlock on employment and continuation that will be hard to break. Proposals made here must in consequence be considered partly a compromise and partly an ideality, a dream that would not be difficult to realize if enough people dreamed it. The requirement of the Ph.D. for tenure or tolerable continuation lies beyond the power of a single discipline to eliminate, although raised voices might have some effect.

Minimum requirements for knowledge of foreign languages also are usually set by units larger than a department, but for literature it is much healthier to require languages for admission than to ask that they be learned during the pinched hours of graduate study. Learning to read and write a second language well can add to wisdom as a smattering of three or four languages, with mastery in none, cannot. For comparative literature or linguistics, a candidate who commands two languages can be trusted to begin a third or a fourth or a fifth.

It is not enough for a man to do the things that be good; but he must also have a care, he do them with a good grace. And a good grace is nothing else but such a manner of light as shineth in the aptness of things set in good order and well disposed one with another and perfectly knit and united together.[1]

The vexed question of the relation of a departmental program or programs for a master's degree to the requirements for the Ph.D. is now confronted variously, depending on the size of the department, the degree of interdepartmental cooperation (e.g., for a Master of Arts in Teaching), and the size and nature of the institution. Usually if the candidate in a special M.A. program in a doctoral university looks in the mirror she sees Cinderella. Few M.A. programs require or allow enough time for reading to prepare a candidate adequately for teaching literature in a college. None of the present flaws in the Ph.D. system can be remedied by settling for any of the current M.A. programs. Look then at a scheme larger than the M.A. for training a college teacher of English and American literature and language.

The first year should include:

1. A course in the principles and methods of advanced literary study. Technical terms that save time in communication need not be avoided. The teacher or texts of this course should identify the kinds of things that can be found out and the methods available for finding them, including the internet on home TV or whatever technology will make available year by year (but not methods of interaction as a substitute for reading). The course will demonstrate the knowledge potential in etymological dictionaries and thesauri. The maxim of learning by doing requires that students submit individual solutions to practical problems.

2. A course in the variety of recent approaches to literary study ("teaching the conflicts," not solely the methods of semiological or literary analysis), all these examined in the context of earlier critical proclamations and theories. I see this not as a history of criticism but as an examination of recent approaches with their backgrounds. Students should be allowed to detect intellectual error. Somewhat as the initial topic in freshman composition has been "my home town," writing in this course can begin and end with "my own home base—and why."

3. A course in which students read primary works (not restricted to a chronological period), engage in oral exchange, and submit critical

papers. As narrative provides a broader foundation than a howl, the literary content might be, for example, narrative poems of identifiable similarities and differences by (a few chosen for particular emphases from) Chaucer, Marlowe (with Chapman), Shakespeare, Dryden or Pope, Swift, Burns, Crabbe, Byron, Tighe, Hunt, Hemans, Keats, Browning, Tennyson, Longfellow, Morris, Masefield, E. A. Robinson, Jeffers, usefully supplemented by choices from Aesop (or John Gay), Ovid, Dante, Gesta Romanorum, the subtle Gottfried von Strassburg, Marie de France, the Mabinogion, Margaret de Navarre, Boccaccio, Goethe, Hugo, Cowper, Jane Taylor, Wordsworth, Frost, Finch, Scott, Shelley, Blake, Trumbull, Whittier, Melville, Arnold, Hood, Aytoun, Barham, Gilbert, Lear, the Rossettis, Poe, Holmes, Langston Hughes, Jeffers, Amy Lowell, Warren, Bogan, Ruth Whitman, Anne Carson, or Southey, Riley, Macaulay. In any event, one or two narratives regarded by the teacher as inferior should be included. Some of the recent refusals of narrative could be usefully allowed to make their point; refusals have received more serious attention in recent histories and studies of poetry than has narrative.

A course of readings in elegy, balladry, or the novella could serve similar comprehensive purposes. Not enough novels could be covered in this introductory course for adequate comparison and contrast of literary devices. Whatever the choices of reading, the course will emphasize devices. Satire, autobiography, confession, or utopias and dystopias for this introductory course could have the value of including both verse and prose. Drama can serve if facilities are available for demonstrating its relation to theater.

This third course will have whatever number of graduate teachers is required for division into small sections, but the readings, if not identical for all sections, should be as comparable as the teachers can sustain with approximately equal competence, and the teachers should remain in communication with each other. If the readings are identical or nearly so from section to section, and the course continues through an academic year, faculty and students will be able to assess one another, will get to know each other better, if teachers exchange sections at midpoint.

4. At or near the end of the first semester (or quarter), an examination, written or part written and part oral, to determine what knowledge and skills, not solely literary but applicable to literary study, each student has accumulated by whatever means. The requirements for each candidate in subsequent academic years will be determined partly by the aims of the individual and partly by deficiences the examination has made apparent. Most candidates who show an awareness only of contemporary writers and current issues, for example, will need to study *Beowulf*, *Piers Plowman*, *The Faerie Queene*, *The Arcadia*, *Volpone*, or *Paradise Lost*, if not all of these. Positive aptitudes rather than deficiencies can be identified for the separation into two paths hereinafter proposed.

5. As an obligation both to apprentice teachers and to undergraduates today and tomorrow, for all graduate assistants there should be workshops in writing, speaking, and guiding. The English department at Stanford has given noteworthy attention to such training of teachers. Apprenticeship to a single senior professor has not served as well when tried in the twentieth as it did in the twelfth century. Not all teachers of rhetoric and logic for freshmen need to study Thomas Aquinas, but all need to be reacquainted as graduate students with rhetoric and grammar.

6. With the proviso that it be literary, what you will, as you like it— *you* meaning departmental consensus or submission to the center of power. To complete the first-year curriculum, a course in a single author could utilize concurrently the values of courses one and two. There may not be room today to require all the traditional "major" authors, but a graduate student of English who does not regard Shakespeare as personally indispensable has chosen the wrong field to teach. If many have been wrong in believing Shakespeare supreme in probing the human heart, he stands as reliable guard at the heart of human language. Literature is made of words, put together in a way to strike a responsive chord.

At one time, most colleges required at the very least as a text Charles Mills Gayley's Classical Myths in English Literature and more often the range in myth of Thomas Bulfinch—classical, chivalric, the peers of Charlemagne. Some institutions offer "The Bible as Literature"; it is surprising how few take into the curriculum even the native American trickster tales, much less the pertinent mythologies of Asia, India, Africa, Teutonic Europe, or, beyond Yeats, the Celts or similar "folk."

In the second, third, and any subsequent years of course work, for the transition toward Utopia here envisioned, a bifurcation to create a road less traveled would best serve curricular reform. For the nonce, call the main road PhDL, for literature, and PhDT the path for technical research. Both will include training and practice in research; both will take chronological order seriously, and neither should encourage candidates to believe that the present changes the past more than the past has affected the present. Such terms as *avant-garde* and *postmodern* lose their last ounce of significance when isolated from the past.

Few who wish to be college teachers should be encouraged to take the narrow path to the PhDT. For the PhDT, close attention to language will be required. Courses with a strong linguistic component, courses in the relation of analytic bibliography to earlier centuries and to recent varieties of language applied belletristically, courses involving current historiography—all such subjects pertinent for comprehensive literary research, including stylistic analysis by computer and the writing of computer programs, should be available departmentally or interdepartmentally for the PhDT. A department that can afford a variety of courses involving linguistic analysis of written or spoken English should require more than one for the PhDT and at least one for the PhDL. Those who prove by performance in the retrograde direction of the PhDT that they have chosen correctly should be supported only rarely by teaching assistantships, rather by scholarships or research assistantships, not royally but as productive members of the commonwealth, destined for libraries, untaxed institutions, corporations, or enterprises interested in books or in precise communication, or as university teachers of their special subjects.

PhDTs will be required to produce "original," useful, acceptable, and defensible dissertations, of a kind regarded by university presses as a book, in language and argument open to comprehension by the widest audience that could be made interested in the subject. By the end of the second year, they should be required to identify the *kind* of dissertation they expect to write, so that they can prepare accordingly in a method, an inspired skill, or a genre, or intensively in interdisciplinary study of a particular chronological period.

No course designed for the PhDT should be closed to candidates for the PhDL. Nor should courses for the PhDL be closed to candidates for the PhDT, but courses organized by genre or theme have less significance for research than for the college teacher of literature. With or without notice of "influence," genre and theme can be presented chronologically. Searches by computer can make courses for the PhDL on a theme—city versus country, independent maidens, landscape into sex, money—seem to include half the universe of writing. Organization by theme need not mean confinement to theme.

For both the PhDT and the PhDL, at least one course in each traditional period, preferably not confined to a single kind such as drama, poetry, or the novel, should at present be available in every academic year. Designers of these courses should be much more alert than their predecessors to writings from Canada, the Caribbean, India and Pakistan, Australia and New Zealand, and other reaches of the English language, and to Asian as well as European and American literatures. A student who prefers period courses to those in genres, methods, or motifs should be encouraged to follow chronological order among periods chosen. As 2001 approaches, every candidate for the PhDL should ideally take at least one course in contemporary writings and one involving a period before 1700 or 1780, one in a genre or kind, one stressing method, and (considering current emphases on race, gender, class) one with gender or ethnic content. Tomorrow's teachers must begin where we are.

Many departments currently require one or more courses before and after 1700 or 1800, but the chief reason for including 1700–1914 in the requirement has been equity for teachers of the rich literatures from that era; students who command the rudiments of literary study have their least trouble in understanding most works of 1700–1914, though they can be led to greater appreciation. What students of literature from 1700 to Conrad, Pound, and Stein primarily need is time for reading incited by examination. Indeed, for any era, and for literature seen in any perspective, the schedule should allow time for reading primary works not discussed in the classroom. The beneficent reading period for undergraduates at Harvard was rendered questionable by commercial cram schools; professors should be close enough to graduate students, and astute enough in writing examinations, to eliminate candidates who misuse time allowed for reading.

Periodization came into being from emphasis on chronology and context, but those elements have through time become more evident in chronological attention to theme or genre—including variations, copulation, detonation, and rejection of genre—than in most courses enclosing isolated periods. Few period courses in recent decades have met the ideal of learning one subject well enough to recognize one's ignorance of all other subjects. Through uniformity of method, periods have become shells occupied by crabs not native to the shells. Declarations of required coursework should encourage the study of subjects offered only in other departments (or programs)—subjects to be included in the general examination of the candidate for PhDL.

It can be expected that all or nearly all courses either will include analysis in class of such elements as structure, tropes, point of view, and methods of characterization or will require the submission of such analysis in writing. If a candidate for the PhDL in the third year cannot be trusted to give a single lecture or preside over a single conference in a course normally taught by a senior professor, the system in that institution needs further reform, including closer supervision of student teaching.

Beginning where we are makes appropriate a course studying particular myths or particular clusters of characters or types of characters traced, for comparison and contrast in technique, through a work of prose, a staged drama, perhaps an opera, and ultimately a movie or video. It is no paradox to say that the greater the incorporation into courses in literature of history, art history, philosophy, psychology, sociology, anthropology, political theory, or film, the greater the importance of freedom for the student to take outside the department, for credit, courses in history, philosophy, film, etc.

Candidates for the PhDL learn to do research, and do it. Their situation is not "look in thy heart and write." They learn and do research to be more reliable as conveyors of knowledge, and equally, of course, to make more reliable anything they publish. Even so, departments of literature have curiously feared to require "creative" writing of graduate students. The world would be improved if every professional student of literature were required to submit a short story, a personal essay, a sonnet, and a "concrete" poem taking a prescribed or nondescript shape—not for a grade but to be checked off as accomplished, like immunization shots required at a customs office.

Seminars, which enable a program to profit from exchanges among students of talent and imagination, might well culminate in inclusive discussion of values and procedures in teaching literature as well as writing about it. *Seminar* and *graduate education* ought to be terms almost synonymous.

The candidate who has completed the courses in the prescribed program for apprentice college teachers then undergoes an oral, or partly oral, departmental or interdepartmental examination that tests strengths in critical acumen, knowledge of the development and fractures of one or more genres, and knowledge of a chosen author worth talking about for twenty or thirty minutes. Other fields examined can again be what you will, as you like it; the candidate's task is to demonstrate that wide reading has been done wide awake. General examinations for the PhDT and PhDL should be equal in length, complexity, and difficulty. If there is to be no dissertation, a portion of the examination should be devoted to the candidate's defense of a piece of writing submitted to demonstrate intellectual strength. With or without a dissertation, an alert institution will require that a professor from outside the candidate's department be the presiding official, whether or not a field from outside the department is examined.

Among reasons that could be offered for requiring a long, sustained dissertation from a college teacher of literature, the most obvious is that employing institutions have a habit of requiring it. My colleagues at Columbia University, accustomed to beginning an interview with "Tell us about your dissertation," were repeatedly confounded by candidates from Rutgers who had lectured to a class of fellow students, in Rutgers' tripartite substitution for a dissertation, but had neither written the required critical essay nor yet decided on the topic of the required research paper. Serious writing should not await the end of course work. Writing ought to be a continuous requirement rather than a final one. To write every day is a surer intellectual test than to write once in a lifetime.

It has not been demonstrated that the capacity to compose a book-length manuscript correlates notably with the ability to teach the morphology of kinds or the comparative anatomy of a random piece of literature, or the value of literary works to an average or above average fellow being. It has been demonstrated that knowledge of methods of research, enhanced in the writing of a dissertation, can be applied successfully in commercial activities by PhDs who failed to secure permanence as teachers. I would not deny the value of writing an acceptable dissertation for the teaching of English in college; I question its value compared with wide reading and consistent, examined performance over a period of three or four years. For many promising teachers the dissertation has been a punishment, or at best an arbitrary hurdle. An early distraction as teacher has been to get the damned thing published.

The beginning teacher has known distraction as apprentice teacher of introductory composition. In the present organization of colleges and universities, those prepared to teach literature begin by teaching freshman composition, a job that eats time as if it were cotton candy. On this subject, advice to the teacher can be rendered ineffective by a supervisor.

It is generally assumed that the holder of a master's degree in English can teach introductory composition. In fact, a supervisor should hold in awe any degree of success. Whether charged with the provisionally admitted or with merit scholars placed in intermediate or advanced courses, the teacher of composition in the student's first year is in the most crucial of all positions for exercising the custodial theory of education. This teacher is on trial for character, is asked to meet standards of intellectual probity students have not required even of their parents (and of course may not have found there); represents the claim of higher education to scrupulosity in the search for truth; disappoints and disillusions by any failure to confess ignorance honestly; registers a strong impression either that higher education is, or that it is not, part of the caring world; is a significant indicator of whether or not learning is fun. If religion, politics, and sex are dangerous subjects for freshman composition, they are so only as tests of the teacher's probity and attention to the job in hand: to improve the form and content of students' writing. Success justifies self-congratulation.

Fortunately for everybody concerned, most students arrive on college campuses with the competency to enter and survive traditional freshman English. As a requirement, "composition rather than literature rules the roost."[2] Regarded as a service course, freshman composition survives to reduce pain among teachers in all fields that require students to submit sentences made of words. These other teachers can better judge accuracy of reading and listening if written answers, prepared or extemporary, in term papers or on examinations, have logic, clarity, proportion, and point. The course must begin, then, in exposition for clarity.

The first writing assignment could be abysmally expository in teaching how to bend language toward the fingers: Write down instructions, to be read to a child, for tying a shoestring. Write clear instructions for assembling a child's toy, a piece of office furniture, or other assemble-it-yourself object, without using a diagram or diagrammatic terms like "Part A" or "Screw B." Really hard problems, such as translating into American English two pages of a software handbook, can wait until later. After one or two expositions as bald as an egg a subsequent assignment could include evaluation: Describe the arrangement of different foods and products on the shelves of a supermarket or grocery nearby, and explain why your proposed modifications to this arrangement would improve it.

In a step beyond the baldly expository, with definition, description, and analysis, it can be shown that comparison, contrast, and analogy provide advantages not only in writing for persuasion but also for disinterested clarity and force. There are always questions of origin: search the internet for the history of shoestrings. And every writer needs to learn early the importance of opening and closing sentences. The first papers by inexperienced writers usually need to be returned for amplification. Before the end of a semester, a larger number of papers may need to be revised for reshaping and reduction to make the argument more compact. Under supervision, reshaping can be accomplished effectively on a word processor.

Guidance in the observation of detail should come early. Have each student describe, for example, the similarities and differences between two houses near the classroom (affluent teachers have been known to pass out tokens for transportation to distant houses), and then assign to classmates X, Y, and Z the task of rewriting the descriptions by A, B, and C for greater accuracy and detail. For fairness and other advantages, a further step adapted from interactive core programs would have the descriptions and evaluations further evaluated in class discussion. Since education and not grade-point average is the aim, examination of the houses in pairs rather than by individuals can produce mutual improvement in observation and expression. If one of the students, or the teacher, can provide architectural terms for components of the houses described, the advantages of an exact professional vocabulary can enter the discussion. Only a dedicated and convinced teacher can convey the joy of entering deeply into the world of language, but she must in every session teach greater care in the handling of words and syntax.

Valid methods of argument should occupy a substantial block of time in any introductory course in writing. The teaching of validity can begin, with some danger to the teacher, by assigning topics likely to expose prejudices livelier than those aroused by the venerable "My Home Town." As politics, sex, and religion cannot be avoided, they may as well be confronted, but no teacher can be sufficiently disinterested to avoid in conscience a declaration of partiality on any issue that arises. The composition teacher's job is not to judge a student's standpoint or conclusion but to identify the apparent methods employed to reach a conclusion. In composition courses teachers in revolt against institutions need to dismount long enough to demonstrate pragmatically some ways that authority is achieved through language.

For practicality, students informed that they are to write reports, not essays, could be taught by experience how, and how not, to do research on buying a car, a computer, a bathroom cleanser.[3] As the mean age of students attending undergraduate courses rises, collaboration between teacher and student and among students will be increasingly appropriate. Even in introductory courses, and even without regard to the increased presence of older students, collaborative writing by several students could serve a range of educational purposes midway through a semester. The first year is too early for the ethnographic writing about peoples and settings successfully instituted for a later year at the University of New Hampshire.[4]

Wherever English departments have the sole or chief responsibility of improving the way first-year students handle words, they have an obligation to argue for the inclusion of imaginative writing. A firm stand for the complexity of language and humanity preserved only in belles lettres—this much they owe to inheritance, to culture, to life. After serving the needs of other disciplines and future employers of the students, teachers can demand tribute to the values of literature. A course in composition can progress from the syllogism through the more informal enthymeme to narrative where the premises of argument are embodied but implicit. In faculty debate on this question, teachers of English and American language and literature have a duty to be convincing (not only to mathematicians and architects but to the less susceptible teachers of engineering and accounting) on the life-enhancing values of imaginative literature for their progeny. The preparation is not for a B.A. or a B.S. but for wholeness, for life.

In the assigned readings, after examples of argument developed as in a classical oration, the next stage might be quasiliterary analysis of such materials already familiar to students as comic strips and situation comedies on television. Wherever English departments have the responsibility for freshman composition, however, teachers should insist on setting, before the end of the course, paradigmatic short stories (or poems, a "Death of the Hired Man"), and these should be made available entire; fragments or samples won't serve. Like the inclusion of current subjects among the expository and argumentative examples, the inclusion of contemporary work brings not only quickening of interest but also, when pointed out, gateways to the represented past. If there is a required textbook for all sections, the individual teacher who believes a contemporary story inferior needs only to tell the class why she as a reader has come to this estimation.

Appropriate readings need to accompany each assignment for writing. As copyright and litigation erect hedges wherever a teacher looks, published textbooks with proper acknowledgments afford a prudent alternative to the use of photocopied materials, whether short stories or a manufacturer's instructions for assembling a toy. But the range of kinds of writing offered as models or dissuasions cannot be too large. Precision, detail, order, proportion, syllogistic progression, tact, energy, suspense, surprise, understatement, irony, point of view, finality, all need to be illustrated and discussed. A book by George G. Williams on creative writing aptly interspersed passages from fiction with such paragraphs as Darwin's meticulous description of the muscles involved as an infant begins to cry. Examples of good writing should be accompanied by examples of bad writing, particularly examples of overwriting. Current journalism has reached a basement so ready to flood that almost any number of any newsmagazine, and most newspapers, afford easy examples of unconsidered argument.

In the 1930s and 1940s introductory courses often included exposure of errors, misrepresentations, prevarications, evasions, anacoluthons, spurious inferences, and other distortions of language in commercial advertisements, particularly in corporate advertising on radio and in magazines. Every course offered in an English department can be improved by the inclusion of contrastive examples of bad writing. Instead of assigning a block of time to false advertising, however, a teacher can more effectively have a cache of examples from newspapers, television, or the internet ready for display when similar errors of logic disfigure student papers.

Assigning E-mail discussion of assigned topics and of each other's initial responses can of course bring a spontaneity and directness of communication between and among students that teachers have traditionally not required. The availability of E-mail has uncovered possibilities of method that existed previously but were overlooked. The temptation now is to choose a crutch taller than the shoulder.

As in courses devoted to literature, a good teacher of composition will know the limits of her knowledge. Admission of ignorance in the classroom is admirable pedagogical practice; the wisest thing a teacher ever says could be, "I don't know," except that a better is "I don't know but will try to find out." Public admission of lack may come hard, but it is much harder and more important to recognize one's ignorance whether the question of admission arises or not. Because a teacher cannot know too much, knowing more than others brings the temptation of enjoying a sense of living as adviser to omniscience. (Handle cautiously information from a Macaulay-like person of apparently infallible memory for tables of numbers or heredity.) Above all, the teacher should know what he does not know. As Cowper put it in *The Task*, "Knowledge is proud that he has learned so much; Wisdom is humble that he knows no more" (6.96–97). A little knowledge is a dangerous thing among teachers largely because the knower thinks it enough for answering any question asked. A teacher who can't bear refrigeration or torpor should get out of the kitchen.

English departments have held a near monopoly on the teaching of freshman composition. They will struggle, when challenged, for the power to designate both the kinds and the names of the teachers, primarily because the course provides employment for graduate students who can be promised upon admission this source of income. Administrations tend to support English in this if in no other cause, because graduate assistants, however reluctantly, furnish the most economical and most predictable and restrainable way of teaching the course. A director of introductory composition staffed by teaching assistants can brandish a moral whip to achieve consistency of standards and methods if not a uniformity of results.

If English departments provide the most practical solution to this vexatious problem, do they necessarily ensure the best result? No. Graduate students in English, despite the odds in their favor, are not necessarily the best writers in higher education and not inevitably the best judges of writing. Selective suggestions for the course have appeared above partly to indicate why departments of English and American literature have been the natural home of freshman composition. So once again, precision, detail, order, proportion, syllogistic progression, tact, energy, suspense, surprise, understatement, irony, point of view, finality—the scope of these virtues can be best absorbed through careful reading of imaginative literature. To what a graduate in French, German, Portuguese, or Russian might bring, the teaching assistant in English can add only a more intensive study of language and literature in English—except an advantage to the institution in the prudent subservience of graduate assistants in English to senior professors in a large department. It is immoral to entice graduate students into supporting advance toward a degree of dubious application by teaching for tuition and a pittance, but it is institutionally economical.

Teaching introductory writing requires an early decision, individual or institutional, concerning the preservation of usages sanctified by writers traditionally regarded as the best. Granted that living languages change, that errors once repellent to philologists and lexicographers descend into common speech, newspapers, and magazines, should teachers of writing seek to maintain venerable distinctions of the kind H. W. Fowler preached in *A Dictionary of Modern English Usage*? My own answer, as a reader who has come this far would expect, is to have it both ways: the teacher of freshman composition, particularly, should avoid coming across as a pedant; toward the other hand, custodians of language have a responsibility to teach usages that augment clarity, but will listen to prudence telling them not to demand or expect precision. (A Fowlerism in that sentence: to *increase* clarity implies that it was previously less clear; to *augment* clarity includes preservation of what has been clear.)5 In any event competent teachers of English will give higher praise to expressiveness than to precision.

Not all debatable changes in language come about through laxity or laziness. The consciousness-raising transformation of *Negro* into the equally inaccurate *Black* did no harm to the American language; feminists matched this semiological change felicitously with *Ms*, but the patriarchal use of *man* to encompass all genders, persistent since *homo* emerged from *humus*, can only be eradicated by a nuclear attack on the language. *Spokespersons* yes, *waitpersons* maybe; *fireman* is a nuisance, with *firefighter* available; *airman* can die of neglect; *chairman* can be regarded as obsolete for *chair*; but *freshpersons*, no, or only to the tonally deaf. Most who say *salesperson* have shied from *salespersonship*. Once consciousness has been raised among the conscious, no great purpose is served by systematically debasing the language in literary works of the past. Our foreparents will not be affected by the rediscovery that their

God lacks gender, but the newer New English Bible will not be improved by substituting *he/she* for *He* throughout, or "they sitteth upon a throne," nor should the Juliet of man-centered Shakespeare cry, "Hood my unperson'd blood!"

We must get used to the once ungrammatical, soon universal "each person should carry their own luggage." The expiring rule of agreement, employing *his*, served no sempiternal purpose. Yet we now get the next step, from eradicating gender to neglecting number, in such clauses as "when a printer shares their technological opinions with you."

Luckily, gender in English is largely a folk memory except in the pronouns, which are now an embarrassing habit like the inherited error of calling "Indians" the native Americans that a policy of genocide failed to obliterate. Nevertheless, among surviving pronouns, *its* can replace *his* or *hers* without comic or ambiguous results only in constructions carefully chosen by the speaker. When pronouns do not distinguish, they intrude. "As they struggled, the girl exerted its will until its forefinger bent like a sapling, exposing its lack of strength." "As they debated, it emerged that its substitution for 'his' lacked the usefulness of the undesired." An unlimited human *its* is not one of the changes we are likely to introduce to the detriment of comprehending literature in English from the Elizabethans until now. Other choices will prevail. As the century turns, the supervisor of freshman composition could best advise teachers to regard *him/her* or *him and her* for *him*, and *their* for *his* or *hers* in a student composition as democratically safe from marks indicating error. Each teacher will have an opinion and can make her opinion known. The accumulated resentment of women asked to teach grammar as subjection to authority will not quickly fade. For others, here's a rule of thumb: correct substandard and ungrammatical language in the papers of those who do not know they are making a choice.

When first-year writing is the subject, the general issue of usage has to be faced. The recent lexicographic solution of permissive inclusion while declaring certain usages "slang" or "substandard" satisfies as many needs as any other compromise. Most teachers with a Ph.D. in English would welcome as a blessed event the presence of a student whose usage had to be marked "obsolete" or "chiefly Irish & Scot." We would all be as happy as kings if we could attain a single national standard of grammar and usage, but that unifying bond, which seemed somehow just barely out of reach when every student had read and read and read Francis Bacon, Charles Lamb, Robert Louis Stevenson, and *The Autocrat at the Breakfast Table*, has never quite existed and will never arrive. The teacher of introductory composition should know the language considered standard between the Appalachians and the Mississippi north of the Mason-Dixon line but has no compelling need to enforce that standard. One need not go as far as Whitman or Faulkner to discover that correctness is not the *sine quâ non* of composition. Yet precision is seldom sinful. Dialectical usage can be tolerated, and on occasion applauded, but only standard American English should be *taught* in freshman composition.

Composition, as a course required for all who do not meet tests of exemption, inevitably suffers from the disadvantage that discipline and performance are reciprocal in the motivation of students. Even total replacements of requirements with electives in various institutions have not stopped cheating; constant suspicion of plagiarism freezes to near zero the pleasure of correcting papers in a required composition factory. The much-berated inflation of grades proceeded in the second half of the twentieth century at a hare's pace, or a rodent's, but in most colleges cheating in large required courses is a greater blight than assigning grades of warped significance. Grades are an outer garment. Even the abolition of grades would not afford relief to the teacher of composition, because a high percentage of students in large colleges have come prepared to cheat themselves by accepting the invitation of assembly-line courses to ignore self-respect.

Student malaise joins other forces that drive the profession into perpetual experiment with the forms and goals of the required course in writing.[6] I have attempted to make particular points, not to describe a course for all seasons.

Although English departments know that their strength in debate derives from possession of required courses in logic and rhetoric, they believe it their mission to be generals and soldiers in the fortress of literary study. They would like to have every student either advance quickly from composition to literature or to begin writing as an adjunct to literary study. The strengths of a good first-year course in composition cannot be matched exactly by a course in common reading and weekly writing taught by representatives from all or several departments in the humanities. Because a required course in the common reading of significant works, if divided into small sections for weekly writing, will tower above the standard composition course for freshmen in enlightenment, the ideal is to have both, as described in the bulletin of the University of Tulsa, where students in the arts and sciences write papers both in writing (rhetoric and logic from the department of English language and literature) and under a member of the senior faculty in a "First Seminar." Multiversities, from intricacies of budget, seldom can accomplish this feat as well as smaller colleges. Centrifugal force in multiversities tends to fling reading away from writing.

By convention and healthy imitation, most colleges have had introductory courses in literature among those that underclassmen are required or encouraged to choose. Failing a core common across the nation, a common core for all students in a single institution beats total choice among electives all hollow. Segregated as a graduate teacher, I came late to the core program of Columbia College in Manhattan. The two basic one-year required courses there, contemporary civilization and literature humanities, have survived change and upheaval all around them since the 1930s. Contemporary civilization was instituted in 1919 when John Erskine returned from teaching issues first of war and then of peace to Yankee soldiers in France. Humanities, the literary companion required since 1937, had its origins in a course taught by George Edward Woodberry and taken by Erskine in the 1890s. Recently a year combining art humanities and music humanities has joined the core of required courses, while Asian and Middle Eastern studies have come to share a requirement with African and other major cultures, with the expected addition of American studies.[7] Colleges elsewhere could more boldly include works from African, Asian, and island cultures within a single required course as core.

Students read in literary humanities at Columbia important works from the *Iliad* to (frequently) Dostoevski, who has given way currently to two works not in translation, Austen's *Pride and Prejudice* and Woolf's *To the Lighthouse*. In contemporary civilization, students consider issues raised by authors from Plato to Nietzsche and Freud (and currently Beauvoir, Hayek, and Rawls) as still apposite. Students submit papers weekly on assigned topics from the reading of the week; the teacher of a section marks these papers and discusses them in class or in conference. From these courses Mortimer Adler under Robert Hutchins at Chicago constructed the programs of Great Books and great ideas and the issue-centered revisions of the *Encyclopedia Britannica*. With the Syntopicon, an index of ideas, joining the fifty-four volumes of Great Books of the Western World, "Culture had finally taken its place," complained Donald McQuade, "as an indexable commodity in a world of consumption."[8] The Chicago packaging has admittedly encouraged many to own ideas without using them.

Issues, ideas, values, and varieties of accomplishment predominate in the Columbia program, but commonalty comes only a step or two behind in significance. Whatever the great books may have been at Chicago under Hutchins, they certainly have not preserved an elite ideology at Columbia. The books speak differently not only to different generations but to each teacher and each student. The books contain issues and values; they do not dictate a response. One who experienced the jar and challenge of the books twice as a student has concluded that the core provides "actually the most radical courses in the undergraduate curriculum."[9] The readings create a commonalty; they stimulate thought but do not control it.

The courses of the core are taught in small sections by seasoned teachers and novitiates, none of them self-selected. Qualified graduate students, each with one section meeting four class-hours a week, are called preceptors, not "assistants"—they alone meet with students in their respective sections. One might think there always has to be a first time, but old hands doubt if anybody should teach a course of such gravity without taking it first. In the spring the entire staff sets the schedule of weekly readings for the following year; the final examination is set by the staff. At Columbia each teacher grades the papers of her own section, a relaxation from traditional Oxbridge scrupulosity and a reduction of the need for teachers to share and teach opinions. Annual inspection of the canon leads occasionally to substitution for the following year of one or two titles; a *Gulliver's Travels* may return from banishment a few years later; a *Malcolm X* tends to fill a revolving slot near the end. Teachers meet at the beginning of each week for discussion of that week's assigned work (normally amounting to an epic, a novel, or three plays) usually with a presentation from a specialist in that corpus. Authority, without a lecturer, resides in the works read, and these are kept open to rational challenge. Most of the teachers are able to maintain a high degree of what is now sometimes condemned as objectivity, enough at least to take the role of devil's advocate against interpretations that seem to be predetermined rather than derived from reading with an open mind.

Normally, under urging, a student will have taken literary humanities in the first year and contemporary civilization in the second. On the campus and in nearby bars, students concur or argue about cruxes in the readings of that week or the previous month. Rather than Great Books easily coaxed into preserving gentlemen's agreements, most of the works read have called readers of each generation into dissatisfaction with self and with unexamined assumptions. Responses to the core demonstrate the pliancy of tradition; most of the works recommend change explicitly, the others implicitly. Until teachers are superseded by robots, the classes will not imbibe "an idea of Culture that is encapsulated into tokens and affixed to curricular charm bracelets to be taken out at parties for display," as one jealous for "the demotic, folk, vulgar, idiosyncratic, ethnic, erotic, black, 'women's,' and genre poetry" has charged of great great Great Books.[10]

Every teacher of a class for upperclassmen at Columbia can expect students to understand allusions to concepts or phrases from the seminal works read in the courses required of all. A Manhattan or Albany lawyer who hears another in the firm allude to idols of the cave with reference simultaneously to Bacon and to Plato recognizes a fellow graduate of Columbia College. Imagine for a moment the value if every sophomore in the United States had read carefully under tutelage the same epics, dramas, satires, and philosophic and political essays— imagine that all had read Montaigne or all had read Alice Walker. Call the required writings masterpieces, great books, important books, good books, or works exerting influence, the requirement brings a common knowledge and shared experience that would be of social value even if the assignments were writings of current interest likely to be ephemeral. In an old Vassar phrase, everything correlates—with a little prodding and shoving.

Commonalty and pursuit of open-mindedness could be achieved by an informed selection of recent works chosen for cultural, geographical, and ideological diversity, including the demotic, folk, vulgar, ethnic, and idiosyncratic—but achieved only among those exposed to this selection. One of the values of selecting from among works long considered readable is the greater likelihood of reaching through them toward a commonalty embracing significant numbers. Across the continent more teachers are likely to vote for *Don Quixote* than for Bellow's *Herzog*.

The purposes expressed in George Washington's will are still valid. He there recommended a national university not only to meet the need for education in arts, sciences, and politics but also that future leaders, he said, "(as a matter of infinite Importance in my judgment) by associating with each other, and forming friendships in their Juvenile years, be enabled to free themselves in a proper degree from . . . local prejudices and habitual jealousies."[11] Not all habitually bickering members of Congress can now be expected to attend the same college, but every step toward a *common* education (as national prejudices will not be "local prejudices") is a step across the nation toward mental and intellectual freedom. Even Gerald Graff's "teaching the conflicts" can be offered as "a common educational experience" within each institution, but graduates would then need to meet others who have had a similar intellectual experience elsewhere.[12] Commonality in higher education would be a partial remedy for the absence from secondary schools and family influence of what E. D. Hirsch Jr. calls cultural literacy, "a common body of knowledge and associations."[13] Nationalism is a virtue when compared with tribalism. The job is not to create an instant commonalty but to identify the commonality that begins in geography and law. Two noble traditions intersect: to join the search for such truth as knowledge can afford, and to persuade in just causes.

Adler's emphasis on issues in the Great Books, which meets a small portion of Washington's aims, can usually achieve its own ends with nonfictional works, from the Declaration of Independence to Freud; it serves less well with the Oedipus plays or Rabelais. The original insistence in the public program of Great Books on no chronology, and no authority or knowledge from discussion leaders beyond the text, cannot distinguish Socrates from Plato. Literary study should include, but cannot be compacted into, issues; in every room of literature, delight awaits the alert reader.

A choice of works in English from Great Britain, Ireland, the United States, Canada, the Caribbean, Australia, New Zealand, India, and many bilingual locations would avoid one objection frequently raised against the Columbia program. As the literary humanities course can draw teachers from a dozen departments and includes translations from Greek, Latin, Italian, French, German, Spanish, and from time to time other languages, few teachers of any one work are adept in the original language of that work. The loss is not merely in pinpoints of meaning but in a galaxy of linguistic skills and nuances. Particularly if students are reading in translation it is preferable to have a teacher who knows the original language. Teachers can consult with colleagues better informed, but consultation cannot cure the need for multilingual competence. In employing teachers not polyglot, something is lost that much may be gained. When challenged in faculty meetings—"Do you think useful value results from reading Dante in translation?"—Erskine answered with a question, "Do you think anything of value can come of reading the authorized King James Version of the Bible?" The dedicated teacher seeks knowledge endlessly, but whole continents of knowledge will fail to outperform, in consequences for education, an awareness of the bordering shore where an ocean of unknowing rolls in against the teacher's knowledge. Here, then, is one chance to debate "the conflicts": Could a strong basic course in literature be devised from works all without translation but from the full range of cultures that have produced writing in English?

The greatest value of literary humanities at Columbia may be its golden reputation.[14] Why do most students in this course climb mountains of reading each week and write about it with personal spark? In most universities the teacher of an institutionwide required course in literature or writing confronts underclassmen who attend grumpily under compulsion. The teacher must ask of every required piece of writing in such courses if any evidence of unexpected superiority results from plagiarism. It is not so in the Columbia core. I drew breath on my first day in Humanities A when the half-expected question that followed a raised hand was "Humanities, okay, but why does it have to be required?" From all sides of the small room, from half of the twenty freshmen assembled for their first day, came assurances that this course would be the greatest experience in that guy's life. Everybody said so. On a Dean's Day, when Edward Said was nominated to expound on the folly of teaching from translation works the teacher could not read in the original languages, in a course aspiring to universality, and a Fellow of the Humanities was nominated to defend a course she was encountering for the first time, parents in the room who had taken the course as given in their time rose to offer testimony as born-again humanists. Such responses account in good part for the impressive stability of the canon in that course and the continuance of a very expensive educational instrument. Word passes from father to daughter.

Cost heads the list of undeclared reasons why Barnard College has declined to sacrifice its alternatives to the core. As Columbia College, still diminutive, continues to admit increasing numbers into its freshman classes, it may conclude that it can no longer afford to provide qualified preceptors for its teacher-intensive core program; the administration looks enviously toward a professor of the humanities lecturing to three or four hundred students, with low-paid assistants doing all but the lectures, as in colleges that juggle guiltily what they call a core program of electives. Colleges that allow electives among basic courses can seek honestly what is hard to come by, the coherence called for by Abraham Flexner in *The American College* of 1908, coherence between the classical core of tradition and free electives. But the highly favorable reputation of the core program at Columbia cannot be achieved through the frequent revisions and reversals in basic requirements that enliven faculty meetings elsewhere. Nor could the Columbia program have maintained its reputation without the frequent meetings of its teachers, who each preside over the discussions and demand thoughtful weekly writing from fewer than thirty students.

The value of commonality, even with its inclusion of justifications for dissent, can be challenged like the Declaration of Independence and the Bill of Rights on the grounds that it does not suffer perpetual revision by dissenters. Columbia makes a twofold claim for its infrequently changed list: that most of the works have impressed many and pleased long, and that the teaching staff as a committee, after listening to students for two semesters, asks whether other works would address as well, or better, significant current concerns. It can be said for the works that have survived such scrutiny that they offer disinterested aid in deciding which current issues are likely to seem significant a decade hence.

The issue of including contemporary works of literature in required or alternative courses bears no basic resemblance to the issues of the multicultural and the global. Contemporaneity has a claim of its own in revealing the reactions of others to where we are together; debate needs to consider only how far contemporaneity more than the past and the different—and mathematics—has to be taught to adults. Teachers of literature have as much responsibility as weekly, monthly, or quarterly reviewers to discover and make known the best works of poetry and imaginative prose coming currently into being. An altogether different question is the opening of windows into alien vistas, current or past.

To those who have taught in the core program at Columbia, something different, a melding of classics from Europe, Middle and Far East, North and South America, all islands, and several world religions would perhaps seem a dilution of the traditional courses refitted with a skimmer. Elsewhere, however, a fresh start could be made by asking how far the Western classics would seem repetitious in content or structure if considered against classics or buried treasures from other cultures, which might replace some portion of the Western for greater contrast. Over several decades English departments arranging courses chronologically have intermixed English and American works only in the latest period; the wisdom and wit of Emerson has not diluted courses in British literature. General anthologies of literature tend to include more translations from contemporary literatures than from earlier periods, a practice that reflects increases in travel, commerce, and communication but includes in only one dimension the distinctly different other. Neither Chaucer nor Milton spent a lot of time imagining Buddhists or Shintoists, but every college graduate today will encounter persons whose classics have not been Western. A full education in the cultural other requires both geographical and chronological distancing. A global culture increases the need for knowledge of the chronological other.

The idea of canon as authority has become a popular cry and favorite target. The estimable Gary Wills offers a perception that George Chapman and Alexander Pope, in keeping with the tastes of their respective times, translated the *Odyssey* with less empathy than the *Iliad*, whereas the taste of our time denies preference to such couplets as "The grisly wound dismiss'd his soul to Hell, / His arms around him rattled as he fell." "So it is not true," Wills concludes, "that the greatest works of art are timeless in their appeal. . . . That is the problem with claims for an immutable canon equally teachable in all times."[15] Leaving aside the assumed proposition that the seventeenth and eighteenth centuries could not or did not appreciate the *Odyssey*, "equally teachable" is a valid term in this context only if given the meaning "teachable in the same way." Although unthinkable for Pope and not the way the *Iliad* was delivered in patriarchal eras, it could today with probity be inquired how far the *Iliad* displays poignantly the fruitless pride and brutality of war. Both Homeric poems will be, the more so in translation, whatever an audience makes of them; but the distinctive powers of construction, metonyny, metaphor, and humanity in each offer pomegranates ready to pluck. You don't think you would like pomegranates. A common error in considering which poems and novels and plays will divert students from visual entertainment is to assume optimum pertinence to current interests from harmony with current tastes. Significant works have most to offer in introducing what has lain outside the reader's awareness. A teacher who cannot find pertinence in the unobserved antithetical has lost the connection between education and educator. Ethnic studies have less value in providing cultural sustenance to what a persuaded student brings to the program than they could have for a student encountering a complete case of otherness. The old philologists were on to more than half a truth: a student has a much better chance of finding without instruction whatever gold there is in this month's immediately acclaimed novel than in making unaided personal use of the treasures within works on display for centuries.

Consider three possibilities for a teacher leading a discussion of a work venerated but without claim to divine authority. One, he can study to transmit received opinion. Two, she can study accumulated opinion but convey reasons arrived at honestly for a new departure or dissent. Three, she can contrive an obliquity that will arouse in students an impulse to flee toward the center.

I go for Two. Concerning Three, Leslie Fiedler has famously declared that the professor is entertainer and neglects that rule at peril. The fundamental need, with or without entertainment, is to awaken. To awaken, effort in preparation should include greater consideration of delivery than I ever mustered, but the aim is to exceed an alarm clock in inducing a durable awareness. Emerson may not have been at his most intoxicating when he said, "Nothing astonishes men so much as common sense and plain dealing," but only elaborately contrived jokes stay with students longer than their measurement of probity in memorable teachers. Moses Hadas, a great awakener, noted that tenfold increases in tuition have made the telling of jokes in class an irresponsible way to awaken. Fiedler's surer way of educating has not been to tell jokes but to startle into attention, a variation on option Three.

The question of entertaining and pleasing in instructional awakening becomes a more contentious issue in the choice of readings, particularly in a core program required of all or most students. Inclusion of contemporary narratives in a traditional core currently displeases both the avid adherents of the Golden Tradition of Great Books, who want no gambling on the contemporary, and tendentious advocates of ethno-American studies, who want more. That education should include a bold look at the present raises the question of whether any contemporary narrative not in some sense ethnic can fully confront the present world of variety and diversity.

The most strident supporters of Great Books attended great multiversities in which core programs were designed against the occupational diversity desired (and paid for) by the financial interests that would like diversity still confined to the occupational: engineering, business, journalism. On the opposite hand, for the near future, the value of incorporating knowledge of ethnic cultures in courses required of all will need to be assessed with sparing attention to its most assertive advocates.

Humanists at Columbia have not predicated an immutable canon for the core. It may be that I have misrepresented the degree of fixity in the college program at Chicago somewhat as Margery Sabin, in defending stability elsewhere, misconstrues the Columbia core as "a humanities curriculum in which universal truths are transmitted to students from on high through the great books of Western civilization."[16] The claim I would make is certainly not for an immutable canon but for a core of works the most likely to provide intellectual and aesthetic stimulus for a considerable proportion of beginning students in colleges of North America. Possibly it is to be lamented that students predestined by family to become national leaders now share the best colleges with a wide range of minds, some sharper and some duller than theirs, but colleges can do no better in any decade than to bring self-knowledge to each individual that society provides. The diversities of society will bring some of the best minds to community colleges and will lodge there some of the wisest teachers. All together need to seek as much common ground as practicable.

More independent colleges than colleges within universities continue to require of all students a survey of literature, British, British and American, or translated from European or world languages. After the survey the curriculum in English, primarily for majors, divides into chronological periods, and most of the few recent appointments to tenure have conformed to that chronological structure. In the Modern Language Association division into periods remains, not at the heart but well above the colon. Periodization continues largely because higher education as we have come to know it requires a specialization in order to display competitively an expertise that survives judgment by peers. The best that has been known and thought becomes the most that has been recently published on the manageable subject of the article you are about to read because you may be able to contest its conclusion. Such specialization does reveal to a teacher degrees of ignorance about other subjects that nonetheless have to be discussed in the classroom.

The multicultural has put heavy, healthful pressure on the slicing of literary study into chronological periods. Why then do most examples in this book concern 1789–1837 in Britain? Simply because as a specialist these are the representative studies I have had the time and opportunity to encounter. We need a new, liberating structure, certainly not one of chronological slivers, as well as new theories.

As for method in classes for upperclassmen, skirmishes and wars over method and theory have not destroyed my preference for the eclectic, call it anecdotal gossip or what you will. Until a better theory is built than any we have now, the eclectic is the road to take. The eclectic in 2001 should not ignore any feasible approaches, including those I have deplored in this volume. Here is a possible sequence for preparation to teach a literary work: Begin by reading the piece (or tome) to discover changes in your own spontaneous response since you last read it. Ask, and then attempt to find out, what the author thought the purposes, the kind, and the distinguishing characteristics of the work to be. Then ask of the work itself how far it agrees with what you understand to be the author's expressed or customary intentions. Regard what it says to you as uncertain. Ponder possible meanings or significance, with dictionary as needed, of individual words and phrases, including the flunky words, *of, by, for, upon*. Distinguish the probable from the possible. Examine the structure, tropes, and rhetorical ploys. Bring all the contexts with which you can become familiar, from genre through visual arts and psychology and sociopolitical history, all that might bear upon interpretation. While entertaining disagreement with received accounts of the work as a possibility, even as a professional opportunity, but not a necessity, ask how far these accounts survive your scrutiny. Ask what else in your being and life has influenced your comprehension and assessment.

Carry this baggage into the classroom with you, but it is not a best step to begin the hour by unpacking it. Begin rather, even in a lecture room, by asking general questions ("How does reading this compare with other experiences you have had this year?"). If you are brimming with too much excitement to begin with questions, explain in a lecture what students should notice and contemplate. Otherwise, after general questions, ask specific questions as if you do not know the answers—because you don't. There is no necessity in literary studies to choose between belief in one immutable truth (or canon) and belief that all propositions are equally true or untrue.

Every teacher will have preferences in content and will find a personal procedure that works better than others. Prepared questions flung out over several hundred heads will seldom encounter a living answer. If students are invited to interrupt a planned lecture, one or more will raise topics the lecturer had expected to save until later. I for one could never find my way back without repetition or omission. Rhetorical skills, native or learned, heighten the power of communication, but educators are wrong who believe content less important than method.

Conference organizers for MLA, considering a range of dogmas from deconstruction to the multicultural, conclude: "There are no transcendent or absolute rules about what belongs in the zone of the literary and in the zone of the nonliterary."[17] If there are precepts for teaching Congreve or Ginsberg other than eclecticism that ranks literature above the critic as lecturer, here may be three: 1. Believe that technical names for literary devices, both old and new, have the virtue only of rapidity and clarity of communication with the previously instructed. 2. Be imaginative in preparation and delivery, but let the cost of tuition influence the content. 3. Utilize all the properties and equipment you please for an audience born into a visual culture, but remain a custodian of literature.

Eclectic choice can serve content as well as method. Comparison of literary works from earlier and later periods has been confined usually to works with parallel structures or a similar configuration of characters, whatever the degree of intention announced by the later writer. In a looser meeting of past and present, appropriation of differing methods, language, assumptions, and apprehensions can be heightened by juxtaposing earlier and later writings without allowing similarities to dominate the choice of works to put before students, somewhat as A. C. Barnes did in acquiring paintings in Philadelphia before he saw how they would fit together in his school and museum. The fewer the similarities, the greater the opportunity for the teacher to identify salient characteristics.

Commitment to the eclectic does not require that more than one method of approach to a literary text or visual image be employed on any day, in any comparison, or in any course. It requires a readiness to pursue possibilities. For some, the bad odor of the eclectic would seem diminished if principles of literary study were declared and acknowledged as sovereign over disciplines eclectically utilized. The eclectic might be purified, not to say flagellated, by a program to reconcile old and new such as Robert Hodge's social semiotics, which would require graduates in literary study to be conversant in semiotics, linguistics, psychology, sociology, and the history of culture and communication of which English literature is a part.[18] None of these disciplines will be entirely foreign to the graduate student in English, on the whole a self-educated lot. The eclectic, recognizing the danger of a little knowledge, asks for risks in acquiring breadth. One version of the eclectic appears in the books of Herbert Lindenberger, where skepticism regarding the efforts of others to "tell us the 'real' history" frees the scholar's imagination for speculative hermeneutics, but without numbing the capacity for archaeological reconstruction of the past, by imaginative examination of documents, scores, engravings, and other materials.

There is no need to hide from sophomores the unknowableness of the past or of meanings, but any theory not employable in eclectic pedagogy is seriously flawed as an educational tool. A reader response theory that excludes what meteorologists think of Shelley's poem "The Cloud" has accepted needlessly narrow assumptions about what poetry is and can do. Meteorologists can belong to an interpretive community. By finding in À la recherche du temps perdu nine rules for self-help, Alain de Botton does not thereby cease to be a reader.

Moral relativism is not rampant among teachers of literature. Timidity is, and the inclination to dent neither fenders nor egos. But if the relativism ascribed to the multicultural has made a morally destructive appeal to adolescents, the secure majority between the Marxist and Hobbesian fringes, who could be dominant if they chose to be, have moral instruments at hand. In courses either of literature or of cultures, teachers can assign works from the vast library of fiction and drama involving moral choice and ask students hard questions about those choices. Education entails learning less than thinking about what one has previously thought. Multiversities possess whole warehouses of moral instruments. Where is the evidence that institutions and faculties frightened by the alleged relativism of the multicultural have considered how interested undergraduates would be in general colloquia on moral judgments and moral decisions? A research university need not be disinterested toward the moral stability of its students. Rationality and truth do not necessarily require all the kinds of objectivity that John Searle asks for; even without objectivity, discovery that a quest for truth is available to call up on the personal screen can be morally stabilizing.

In teaching literature, there are places for genre, mode, structure, borrowings and transformations, surprises, context of what is present or significantly absent, focus, schemes, tropes, icons, kinds of narrator, tenses, tensions, carnival, audience, intention, influence, psychology, significance of both edifying and ethical sorts, and *moment* in an individual life, in literature, and in consciousness ("science")—these not to exclude literary characteristics yet to be defined. The teacher will not achieve or claim expertise in all directions. The critic who writes for colleagues as if omniscient can relinquish omniscience in the classroom. Eclectic need not imply that all procedures are equal. Depending upon temperament, one committed to teaching will convey, however unconsciously, either a passionate determination ("advocative") to make justice prevail in the classroom and in the world or a firm commitment, from internal integrity, to the clarification ("objective") of such concepts as justice.

Even in separating graduate study for research from study for teaching, I insist on their singleness of purpose. Professor Louis Menand of the City University of New York grants that "the criticism of literature has, of all the major fields of study, the weakest case for inclusion in the professional structure of the research university."[19] The popular view that most "literary research" is useless is modified by proponents of undergraduate education to "essentially useless."[20] They exaggerate. Scholars of language and of literatures perform research that changes knowledge significantly: linguistic theory and analysis, production of reliable editions, biographies, bibliographies, bibliographic analysis and description, morphology, definition, description, justification, discoveries and promulgations of writings that deserve attention, surveys of new fields and methods, including the conception and inventive programming of technical devices to aid in some of those activities. Teachers trained as researchers have helped students see how language and society interact, how one reader's perceptions can be modified by how the author, the work, and readers of diverse assumptions have interacted. Unpredictable innovative ideas in theory and critical method will motivate and compel teachers equal to those now engaged in these tasks. Personal culpability reminds me to urge once more that these scholars begin to speak to a wider audience.

I conclude of literary study what Vaclav Havel concludes of tribes and religions:

> And so far, it would seem that the more tied the various civilizations, cultural and religious groups are by the bonds of a single global civilization—exerting unavoidably a unifying influence—the more they emphasize their sovereignty, inalienable identity, specificity or simply things by which they differ from the circle of the other groups. It's as if one lived in an epoch of accentuated spiritual, religious and cultural "otherness." This growing accent is indeed another large threat to this world. . . . I have gained the indelible impression that they have

much more in common than they admit or are willing to admit. . . . Is it within the power of wise people to bring about . . . recovery or revolution by their own will and by cooperation without the need for any appalling impulse from the outside?[21]

Henry Louis Gates Jr. speaks for me on commonalty. Humanism "asks what we have in common with others while acknowledging the internal diversity among ourselves. It is about the priority of a shared humanity."[22] Among and within humanists, tensions will continue—people are no damn good, all have gone astray, every individual is precious, all life is either sacred or interdependent, leave me alone, love the little platoon, poetry and fiction make shit beautiful, knowledge of reality is illusion but truth and justice and charity remain as necessities—within these tensions literary works available for study attempt to reduce irresoluble mysteries to a negotiable maze.

It is not as critics, but as conscientious custodians, restorative curators, propagators, and propagandists of literature—as close scholarly readers and as scholarly examiners of words and literary artifacts—that professors of literature will continue to earn an honorable place in higher education. In literary study devotion should be paid to the supreme being that inspired Augustine, Alexander Pope, and Voltaire. Literature is useful for a skeptical conduct of life. It is a life-enhancing part of life.

Examples of Management

Nobody, as Vincent Scully says of Yale, can believe the figures supplied by the managers of higher education to national collectors of statistics concerning education. Information in this appendix has been garnered principally from directories and bulletins.

In 1992–93 the relatively lean University of Texas at Austin, with students held slightly under fifty thousand, had a President, six Vice Presidents, and seventeen Deans, most with five or more Associate and Assistant deans. Among the scores of "Offices," each with several rooms, desks, telephones, computers, and office chairs—and not counting the physical offices of teaching Departments, open to students—the Bureau of Economic Geology typically listed two Associate Directors, two Acting Associate Directors, and four Deputy Associate Directors. Associates and Assistants in the scores of Offices required further secretaries and assistants. "What we want to do and must do," says Edwin R. Sharpe Jr., MBA, the Vice President for Administration and Public Affairs, "is operate the University from the management standpoint in the most enlightened possible way."[1] Management presides over two groups: employees and "customers."

By 1994–95 there were seven Vice Presidents, and by 1996–97 eight, with corresponding increases generally, although the Bureau of Economic Geology had economically reduced the number of Associate Director positions from four to three. Officers in academic computing services grew from three to twelve, with administrative computing services adding seven more. Officers in Accounting increased from ten to fourteen.

These in the university at Austin. Above them, the University of Texas System had in 1993 a Chancellor, three Executive Vice Chancellors, four other Vice Chancellors, and more than thirty additional Executive Directors, Directors, and other officers of status requiring assistants. And no students. By 1996–97 the Vice Chancellor for Asset Management had given way to three vice presidents and two managers in a separate company. Above these, a board of appointed regents for each of several university systems in the state; further above, commissioners to adjudicate the competing claims of the several systems. Under the Texas Higher Education Coordinating Board, the University of Houston has become a complex system extended beyond the city's borders. Above all (except a governor's veto) the state legislature, with monkey wrenches ready. The governor appoints; the legislature monitors.

As of 1995, the University of Wisconsin at Madison, one of fifteen centers each with a Chancellor, announced forty thousand students (seven-tenths of them undergraduates), 2,284 total faculty, 5,403 academic staff, 7,671 classified unacademic staff, with 21,199 employees. A Chancellor (with an office of thirteen) and three Vice-Chancellors. The offices of bursar, budget, and business services list 37 officers, including three Assistant Vice Chancellors. The Division of Information Technology lists about sixty telephone numbers. Schools, colleges, and some departments, for example chemistry, have their own administrative, purchasing, and payroll sections. In 1954, on the membership card of an organization opposed to Senator Joseph McCarthy, a member of the growing administration presciently identified himself as "Associate Dean No. 1." Partly housed in Madison, the university system has a President and (counting the Provost at Madison) five Vice Presidents. Above the system, the Board of Regents, the governor, and the legislature. The result, as in other states, is a striated version of chaos.

In Columbia University, private or at least not state-operated, the number of titled officers in central administration grew at the normal rate between 1991–92 and 1996–97, from over 475 to over 500, with 2,300 officers overall. With titles juggled, eleven Vice Presidents increased to thirteen; a Provost and three Vice Provosts presided over twenty-eight Deputy, Associate, and Assistant Vice Presidents in 1991, and over forty in 1996, with the payroll office only knows how many Directors, Associate and Assistant Directors, and assistants to the Associate Directors. Some 203 officers under the Provost in 1991 had by 1996 become 134 under the Provost and 192 under an Executive Vice President for Administration, with a rearranged financial division reduced from 85 to 46. When readjustment brings a new title, however, even with temporary reductions in numbers, expect a gradual competitive increase under that head. Divide an office, and the numbers will soon double. Vice Presidents vie in inefficiency to increase power in the hierarchy by acquiring additional employees. In 1997 Columbia added a Vice President for Facilities Management, supervising fifty-six buildings and reporting to the Executive Vice President for Administration for "more than 475 University employees."[2]

Penn State, with more than twenty locations and twenty-seven or more development officers, seems to keep prestigious titles down to one Executive Vice President and Provost, five Senior Vice Presidents, and among the eleven General Officers only four Vice Presidents, with, as Abe Burrows had it, "heaven knows how many kilowatts."[3] Twenty Deans and their aids represent educational complexity at Penn State. Tellingly, in 1995–96 the Center for Academic Computing had eighty-six identified employees, and the Office of Telecommunications fifty-one. And congressmen in 1991 expressed surprise that central administrations absorbed on average two-thirds of federal funds provided for research!

In 1995–96, under the regents of the University of California system, with a general counsel of thirty lawyers, the system had a President, two Senior Vice Presidents, three Vice Presidents and one Vice

Provost, four Associate Vice Presidents, and eight Assistant Vice Presidents. Among the 170 or so titled officers, the large numbers begin with the directors, managers, and assistants to each officer. A senate of faculty and administrative officers is given authority to determine academic policy for the nine campuses (with 162,300 students). The oldest of the nine, Berkeley, with about 30,000 students, had a Chancellor, five Vice Chancellors, and about 300 titled officers, including 22 Deans and fully distributed Associates and chief Assistants. UCLA, with more than 23,000 of its nearly 40,000 students in the College of Letters and Science (with a faculty of 800), a Chancellor, Assistant Chancellor, Executive Vice Chancellor, nine Vice Chancellors (two ranked between Vice and the Associate Vice Chancellor), twelve Assistant Vice Chancellors, with deans, directors, Deputy Assistant Vice Chancellor, Chief-of-Staff, executive officers, and coordinators among the 240 or so titled officers.

Stanford University, with 14,044 students and a declared faculty of 1,456 in 1995, had in 1996–97 an Executive Vice President for Real Estate (under a Chief Executive Officer for the management company), three Senior Vice Presidents, seven Vice Presidents, a Provost, six Vice Provosts, two Senior Associate Provosts, three Associate Provosts, two Associate Vice Provosts, and forty-eight Directors. By intermixing under these the deans, associates, and assistants, from student affairs to children's hospital, Stanford might find it harder than other universities to declare the deans' offices, in a public accounting, as educational rather than administrative expense.

The University of Tulsa in 1996 had 4,500 students; faculty of 340 including Instructors but not counting Adjuncts; 7 chief Administrative Officers; 44 other Administrators, including two Associate Vice Presidents and one Assistant Vice President; more than 60 in central offices of business operations, budget, finance, and development; fewer than average in undergraduate admissions (19), registration (6), personnel (11) and employment (4), with representative numbers in athletics (55), McFarlin Library (70), computing and information services (31). As elsewhere, two score administrative offices represent the complexity of the university and of the society it serves.

By 1994 Rice University had "a president, a provost, six vice presidents, nine academic deans, a director of the Baker Institute, a dean of students and a dean of admissions—double the number of administrators thirty years earlier."[4] In 1996, with five Vice Presidents and about ninety administrative officials, Rice improved the office of Dean of Graduate Studies to Vice Provost for Research and Graduate Studies, lost the rank of Dean of Students, gained an Associate Vice President for Student Affairs, and added one Associate Provost and one Assistant Provost.

At Lawrence University, a slender and sparing college with a Conservatory of Music, the Vice President for Business Affairs and Administration had in 1996–97 sixteen assistants of various rank, the Vice President for Development and External Affairs twenty; an Admissions Office of eighteen (ten named in the course catalog)—increased, as everywhere, for recruiting. Departments of the humanities housed in Main Hall shared a secretary. Even chaste Reed College, with one Dean of the Faculty and one Executive Vice President, has elevated two other officers to Vice President; the business office employs nine, computing and information services nineteen.[5] Bennington College, forced to reduce faculty as a way to save the institution, has a single Vice President for Finance and Administration and a Director of Development.

In the 1960s the bulletin of a green college in the Northwest announced the reduction of all faculty titles to "teacher" and what other schools ranked as freshman, sophomore, etc., to "student," but the administration was hierarched under the President as Associate, Assistant, and Assistant to the Associate. This is higher education.

PREAMBLE

1. Carla Hesse, "Humanities and the Library in the Digital Age," in *What's Happened to the Humanities?*, ed. Alvin Kernan (Princeton, N.J.: Princeton University Press, 1997) 108.

2. Wendell V. Harris, "The Discourse of Literary Criticism and Theory," *Social Epistemology* 10.1 (1996): 75–88.

3. Throughout, *Ph.D.* indicates the degree, *PhDs* the holders of this degree.

ONE. FROM ANCIENT CLASSICS TO MODERN

1. George Washington, "Last Will and Testament," in *Writings*, ed. John Rhodehamel (New York: Library of America, 1997) 1026. A change in the meaning of *literature* introduced by the Romantics, from "learned" to "imaginative," is noted by Raymond Williams, *Keywords: A Vocabulary of Culture and Society* (New York: Oxford University Press, 1976) 150–54.

2. *Life of Henry Wadsworth Longfellow*, ed. Samuel Longfellow, 2 vols. (Boston: Ticknor, 1886) 1:266.

3. Longfellow 2:184.

4. John Milton, "Of Education," in *Complete Poems and Major Prose*, ed. Merritt Y. Hughes (New York: Odyssey, 1957) 632, 631.

5. When John Winthrop assumed the Hollis Professorship in Mathematics and Natural Philosophy at Harvard in 1738, he required both a longer telescope and a

laboratory of experimental physics: Frederick Rudolph, *The American College and University: A History* (New York: Knopf, 1968) 28–29; Samuel Eliot Morison, *Three Centuries of Harvard, 1636–1936* (Cambridge: Harvard University Press, 1936) 80, 92–93.

6. Rudolph, *American College* 31–41.

7. George Washington, *Writings* 1026.

8. Daily themes at Harvard survived until the monotony "drove Robert Frost out of College."—Charles H. Grandgent, "The Modern Languages," in *The Development of Harvard University Since the Inauguration of President Eliot, 1869–1929*, ed. Samuel Eliot Morison (Cambridge: Harvard University Press, 1930) 70.

9. For recorded debates in literary societies of one college, see David M. R. Culbreth, *The University of Virginia: Memories of Her Student Life and Professors* (New York and Washington: Neale, 1908).

10. E. Merton Coulter, *College Life in the Old South* (Athens: University of Georgia Press, 1928) 66–81; a recurrent subject in Morison, *Three Centuries*, indexed as "Student life."

11. Morison, *Three Centuries* 25–26, 81, 261.

12. For McCosh's attack see *American Higher Education: A Documentary History*, ed. Richard Hofstadter and Wilson Smith, 2 vols. (Chicago: University of Chicago Press, 1961) 2:715–30.

13. Morison, *Three Centuries* 344, 365, 389.

14. George Wilson Pierson, *Yale College: An Educational History, 1871-1921* (New Haven: Yale University Press, 1952) 47.

15. An exception may be the University of Wisconsin, where cheating was the major continuous problem until the 1880s and the 1920s, and after those peaks of misconduct: Merle Curti and Vernon Carstensen, *The University of Wisconsin: A History*, 2 vols. (Madison: University of Wisconsin Press, 1949) 1:382–84, 416–17, 547–48, 672–78; 2:140–41, 525–32.

16. Winton U. Solberg, *The University of Illinois, 1867–1894* (Urbana/Champaign: University of Illinois Press, 1968) 9–10, 274–85.

17. Claude Moore Fuess, *Amherst: The Story of a New England College* (Boston: Little, Brown, 1935) 253–54.

18. Clark Kerr, *The Use of the University* (Cambridge: Harvard University Press, 1964; 2nd ed. New York: Harper & Row, 1972); Christopher J. Lucas, *American Higher Education: A History* (New York: St. Martin's, 1994) 313. The request for the charter of Cornell in 1865 promised "the cultivation of the arts and sciences and of literature, and the instruction in agriculture, the mechanic arts and military tactics, and all knowledge."—quoted in Morris Bishop, *A History of Cornell* (Ithaca: Cornell University Press, 1962) 64.

19. Rudolph, *American College* 400.

20. It can be argued that the "teaching of English literature . . . promised to serve as a binding principle for Americans" who had been divided before and then by the Civil War.—Gerald Graff and Michael Warner, *The Origins of Literary Studies in America: A Documentary Anthology* (London and New York: Routledge, 1989) 5.

21. Susan T. Hill, *The Traditionally Black Institutions of Higher Education, 1860 to 1982* (Washington, D.C.: National Center for Educational Statistics, 1984) ix-xii; Antoine Garibaldi, ed., *Black Colleges and Universities: Challenges for the Future* (New York: Praeger, 1984) 3–5; Julian B. Roebuck and Komanduri S. Murty, *Historically Black Colleges and Universities: Their Place in Higher Education* (Westport, Conn.: Praeger, 1993) 36.

22. Morison, *Three Centuries* 103.

23. Robert Samuel Fletcher, *A History of Oberlin College from Its Foundation Through the Civil War* (Oberlin: Oberlin College, 1943) 1:120.

24. Rudolph, *American College* 323.

25. Ellen Fitzpatrick, *Endless Crusade: Women Social Scientists and Progressive Reform* (New York: Oxford University Press, 1990) 84.

26. Data from the NYU dissertation of John S. Lewis, repeated in Kermit Vanderbilt, *American Literature and the Academy: The Roots, Growth, and Maturity of a Profession* (Philadelphia: University of Pennsylvania Press, 1986) 84.

27. Donald McQuade, "Intellectual Life and Public Discourse," in *Columbia Literary History of the United States*, ed. Emory Elliott et al. (New York: Columbia University Press, 1988) 718.

28. Abraham Flexner, *Universities American, English, German*; reissued with an introduction by Clark Kerr (New Brunswick: Transaction, 1994) 30–31.

TWO. FROM LANGUAGE TO CONTEXT

1. Catherine Gallagher, "The History of Literary Criticism," *Daedalus* 126.1 (1997): 139.

2. William Stanley Jevons, *The Principles of Science: A Treatise on Logic and Scientific Method*, 2 vols. (London: Macmillan, 1874) 1:ix; Thomas H. Huxley, "The Progress of Science, 1837–1887," *Methods and Results: Essays* (London: Macmillan, 1893) 65.

3. William Harmon, "English Versification: Fifteen Hundred Years of Continuity and Change," *Studies in Philology* 94.1 (1997) 2.

4. Stipulation by the faculty that book value would remain unchanged, in wait for better times, lost meaning in the inflation after World War II.

5. William H. Honan, "Scholars Shaking Shackles of Cumbersome Footnotes," *Austin American-Statesman* 18 August 1996: A26.

THREE. THE GROWTH OF CARE IN METHOD

1. "Diversity and Learning," *The President's Report, 1993–1995* (http://www.harvard.edu/presidents office); abbreviated as "The Uses of Diversity," *Harvard Magazine* (March/Apr. 1996): 49–62.

2. Hugh Davis Graham and Nancy Diamond, *The Rise of American Research Universities: Elites and Challenges in the Postwar Era* (Baltimore, Md.: Johns Hopkins University Press, 1997) 27.

3. Denis Donoghue, "The Practice of Reading," in *What's Happened to the Humanities?*, ed. Alvin Kernan (Princeton, N.J.: Princeton University Press, 1997) 122–40.

4. Michael Wood quotes in a single paragraph Blackmur, "An author should remember, with the Indians, that the reality of a word is anterior to, and greater than, his use of it can ever be," and Davie, "It is language which happens through the speaker, not the speaker who expresses himself through language."—"Literary Criticism," in *Columbia Literary History of the United States*, ed. Emory Elliott et al., (New York: Columbia University Press, 1988) 1009–10.

5. "The Uses and Abuses of Literature at the Modern Language Association Conference," *Academic Questions* 1:1 (1987–88): 38.

6. Hilary Putnam, "A Half Century of Philosophy," *Daedalus* 126.1 (1997): 196.

7. George H. Douglas, *Education without Impact: How Our Universities Fail the Young* (New York: Birch Lane, 1992) 70.

8. Verbal report by William Nelson, then president of the Renaissance Society of America.

9. "Describing Poetic Structures," *Yale French Studies* 36/37 (1966): 200–42; reprinted in *Structuralism*, ed. Jacques Ehrmann (Garden City, N.Y.: Doubleday Anchor, 1970).

10. Peggy Kamuf has something original and significant to say in *The Division of Literature or the University in Deconstruction* (Chicago: University of Chicago Press, 1997), but she says it only to those trained in the composite language of theory from France.

FOUR. DISRUPTION, DECONSTRUCTION, AND DIASPORA

1. "The University and Personal Life: Student Anarchism and the Educational Contract," in *Higher Education: Demand and Response*, ed. W. R. Niblett (San Francisco: Jossey-Bass, 1970) 51. James Jarrett's response blamed student unrest on rigid grading, examinations, and the mushy curriculum in general education (52).

2. Frustrated desire, the end of a need for deferred gratification, and the liberation movements of the Third World are recurring topics in Ronald Fraser et al., *1968: A Student Generation in Revolt* (New York: Pantheon, 1988), a collection of memories gathered in an oral history project.

3. Catherine Gallagher, "The History of Literary Criticism," *Daedalus* 126.1 (1997): 145.

4. "Crimson Tide," *Wall Street Journal* 17 March 1997: A18, reviewing Roger Rosenblatt's elegiac account, *Coming Apart: A Memoir of the Harvard Wars of 1968* (Boston: Little, Brown, 1997).

5. Kevin P. Keim, *An Architectural Life: Memoirs & Memories of Charles W. Moore* (Boston: Little, Brown, 1996) 112.

6. David Damrosch, "A Past We Can Live With," *Civilization* 4.2 (1997): 78. I should think that the heightened complexities in theorizing have come from increasing competition among PhDs for differentiated topics rather than from Damrosch's attribution to "the demographic shifts that have brought more women and more minority students into the classroom."

7. Luc Ferry and Alain Renaut, *La Pensée 68: Sur l'anti-humanisme contemporain* (Paris: Gallimard, 1985), on "le Nietzschéisme français," "la dissolution de l'idée de vérité," "les morts du sujet."

8. "Three Ways of Reading," *Bulletin of the American Academy of Arts and Sciences* 51.5 (1998): 36–47.

9. In *The Future of Academic Freedom*, ed. Louis Menand (Chicago: University of Chicago Press, 1996) 24, 31.

10. James L. Kastely, *Rethinking the Rhetorical Tradition* (New Haven: Yale University Press, 1997) 13: "Having recognized a radical indeterminacy, it offers the comfort of an earned and relatively stable closure."

11. Here from *Austin American-Statesman* 21 July 1997: A9.

12. Joseph Marusiak, letter quoted in *Final Report, MLA Committee on Professional Employment* (1997): 26.

13. James H. Pickering and Jeffrey D. Hoeper, *Literature* (New York: Macmillan, 1982) 3.

14. William H. Pritchard, *Frost: A Literary Life* (New York: Oxford University Press, 1984) xiii.

15. Review of John Halperin, *The Life of Jane Austen* (Baltimore, Md.: Johns Hopkins University Press, 1984), in *Times Literary Supplement* (London) 2 August 1985: 859.

16. The examplar I take to be Peter Sellars, but a single number of *Opera News* (62.10 [1998]) includes a complaint by Joel Honig—"The will of the composer and librettist has been broken, the warped sensibility of opportunistic shysters is interpreting its provisions, and the audience is disinherited; the fortune it was bequeathed is tallied in counterfeit bills" (21)—and praise of Sellars by the conductor Andrew Davis as among directors having "the greatest respect for the music and have not wanted to violate it in any way" (15).

17. For a valuable discussion of New Historicism and a list of readings, see Wendell V. Harris, *Dictionary of Concepts in Literary Criticism and Theory* (Westport, Conn: Greenwood, 1992) 147–52. In this book, in *Interpretive Acts* (Oxford: Clarendon, 1988), and in other studies, Harris has thrown light on "an ever increasing mass of literary theory intelligible to an ever shrinking number of readers."—"The Discourse of Literary Criticism and Theory," *Social Epistemology* 10.1 (1996): 75.

18. Graff and Warner, *Origins of Literary Studies in America* 12–14.

19. Edward Sarmiento, in *Cassell's Encyclopaedia of Literature*, ed S. H. Steinberg, 2 vols. (London: Cassell, 1953) 1:69, 517; 2:1921, 1936.

20. Dorothy James, "Bypassing the Traditional Leadership: Who's Minding the Store?"in *Profession* 1997 (New York: Modern Language Association of America, 1997) 41–53. Russell A. Berman in the same volume, 61–74, argues that cultural approaches remain closer to language than do strictly literary approaches in an era of theory.

21. There is a further list of jeremiads in Lawrence W. Levine, *The Opening of the American Mind: Canons, Culture, and History* (Boston: Beacon, 1996) 3.

22. There is a relatively disinterested survey of detractors and doom-sayers of 1986–1993 in Christopher Lucas, *American Higher Education* 269–97, but heavy barrages continue to hold down friendly troops.

23. *English as a Discipline; or, Is There a Plot in This Play?*, ed. James C. Raymond (Tuscaloosa: University of Alabama Press, 1996) 11–28.

24. University and corporate executives in 1997 made reduction of departmental autonomy one goal in "Breaking the Social Contract: The Fiscal Crisis in Higher Education," issued by the Commission on National Investment in Higher Education, convened by the Council for Aid to Education, a subsidiary of the Rand Corporation.

25. Alvin J. Schmidt, *The Menace of Multiculturalism: Trojan Horse in America* (Westport, Conn.: Praeger, 1997) 3.

26. "Postmodern Culture," in *The Columbia History of the American Novel*, ed. Emory Elliott (New York: Columbia University Press, 1991) 518.

27. David Sacks and Peter Thiel, "Multiculturism and the Decline of Stanford," *Academic Questions* 8.4 (1995): 61.

28. *U.S. News and World Report* 21 July 1997: 14.

29. Isaiah Berlin, *The Sense of Reality: Studies in Ideas and Their History*, ed. Henry Hardy (London: Chatto and Windus, 1996) 170.

30. Phyllis Frus and Stanley Corkin in Raymond, *English as a Discipline* 119–42.

31. Einar Haugen *The Ecology of Language*, ed. Anwar S. Dil (Stanford, Calif.: Stanford University Press, 1972) xiv, 3.

32. Karl Kroeber, *Ecological Literary Criticism: Romantic Imagining and the Biology of Mind* (New York: Columbia University Press, 1994) 1. Romantic studies provide a natural point of departure; see also Jonathan Bate,

Romantic Ecology (London: Routledge, 1991); Cheryll Glotfelty and Harold Fromm, eds., *The Ecocriticism Reader: Landmarks in Literary Ecology* (Athens: University of Georgia Press, 1996); and the "Green Romanticism" number of *Studies in Romanticism* 35.3 (Fall 1996).

33. Willard Spiegelman, *Majestic Indolence: English Romantic Poetry and the Work of Art* (New York: Oxford University Press, 1995) 155.

34. Francis Oakley, "Ignorant Armies and Nightime Clashes," in *What's Happened to the Humanities?*, ed. Alvin Kernan (Princeton, N.J.: Princeton University Press, 1997) 73 and notes, 81.

35. "A Dickens of a Theory," *Newsweek*, 3 Feb. 1997: 8.

36. *ARTnews* 96.1 (1997): 104, 102.

37. "The Latest Casualty," *Wall Street Journal* 23 Jan. 1997: A18.

38. Paul F. Lazersfeld and Wagner Thielens Jr., *The Academic Mind: Social Scientists in a Time of Crisis* (Glencoe, Ill.: Free Press, 1958) 14.

39. William H. Honan, "The Ivory Tower Under Siege," *New York Times* 4 Jan. 1998, 4A: 33.

40. Francis Oakley, "Ignorant Armies" 73. On other diminutions noted in this paragraph, see in the Kernan volume, Lynn Hunt, "Democratization and Decline? The Consequences of Demographic Change in the Humanities," 17–31; John H. D'Arms, "Funding Trends in the Academic Humanities, 1970–1995," 32–60; Carla Hesse, "Humanities and the Library in the Digital Age," 107–21; and graphs in the appendix, 245–58. Hunt worries that charges of "feminization" will continue to damage humanistic disciplines (28–29).

FIVE. THE SURROUND

1. Susan H. Russell et al., *Faculty in Higher Education Institutions: 1988* (Washington, D.C.: US Department of Education, 1990) 45, cited in Francis Oakley, "The Elusive Academic Profession," *Daedalus* 146.4 (1997): 49.

2. David Damrosch, *We Scholars: Changing the Culture of the University* (Cambridge: Harvard University Press, 1995) 189, 204–5.

3. Donald Kennedy, "Making Choices in the Research University," *Daedalus* 122.4 (1993): 147.

4. Frederick Rudolph, *The American College and University: A History* (New York: Knopf, 1968) 405, 404.

5. Lewis H. Miller Jr., "Bold, Imaginative Steps Are Needed to Link Teaching with Research," *Chronicle of Higher Education* 13 Sept. 1989: A52.

6. Michael Bérubé and Cary Nelson, eds., *Higher Education under Fire: Politics, Economics, and the Crisis of the Humanities* (New York: Routledge, 1995) 15.

7. Robin Wilson in *Chronicle of Higher Education* 20 Dec. 1996: A10.

8. Patricia J. Gumport, "Public Universities as Academic Workplaces," *Daedalus* 126.4 (1997): 124.

9. Page 7. In light of management's solution of costs by continuous reduction in full-time, continuing teachers, the MLA committee is understandably reluctant to recommend "across-the-board" reductions in graduate enrollments (23).

10. "Retaining Faculty Lines," *Profession 1997* (New York: Modern Language Association of America, 1997) 56–57.

11. William G. Bowen and Julie Ann Sosa, *Prospects for Faculty in the Arts and Sciences: A Study of Factors Affecting Demand and Supply, 1987 to 2012* (Princeton, N.J.: Princeton University Press, 1989) 17, 19; Francis Oakley, "The Elusive Academic Profession: Complexity and Change," *Daedalus* 126.4 (1997): 52; 64 n. 31.

12. *Chronicle of Higher Education* 2 Sept. 1996: 24.

13. *The End of Mandatory Retirement: Effects on Higher Education*, ed. Karen Holden and W. Lee Hansen (San Francisco: Jossey-Bass, 1989) 85–95. Matthew W. Finkin points out that Ruebhausen's solution of contracts for "a long but fixed duration" does not resolve the legal questions and would ask all college teachers to enter the profession on probation until age fifty or older with the assumption of dismissal (97–111). Finkin then recommends that institutions modify annuities and other pension policies to discourage prolonged service (110).

14. Cheryl B. Leggon, "The Scientist as Academic," *Daedalus* 126.4 (1997): 233.

15. Richard Hofstadter and Walter P. Metzger, *The Development of Academic Freedom* (New York: Columbia University Press, 1955) 86, 88.

16. Samuel Eliot Morison, *Three Centuries of Harvard, 1636–1936* (Cambridge: Harvard University Press, 1936) 69–75, 159–60.

17. Thomas L. Haskell, "Justifying the Rights of Academic Freedom," in *The Future of Academic Freedom*, ed. Louis Menand (Chicago: University of Chicago Press, 1996) 48–53.

18. Christopher J. Lucas, *American Higher Education: A History* (New York: St. Martin's, 1994) 305.

19. Louis Joughin, *Academic Freedom and Tenure* (Madison: University of Wisconsin Press, 1967) 143–46.

20. Jane Sanders, *Cold War on the Campus: Academic Freedom at the University of Washington, 1946–1964* (Seattle: University of Washington Press, 1979) 39, 79–86.

21. "Academic Tenure and Academic Freedom," in *Freedom and Tenure in the Academy*, ed. William W. Van Alstyne (Durham, N.C.: Duke University Press, 1993) 344.

22. Quoted in Van Alstyne, ed., *Freedom and Tenure in the Academy* 326.

23. Edmund L. Pincoffs, ed., *The Concept of Academic Freedom* (Austin: University of Texas Press, 1972) x; Joan W. Scott, "Academic Freedom as an Ethical Practice," in Menand, ed., *Future of Academic Freedom* 166.

24. Sweezy vs. New Hampshire, 354 U.S. 234, 250 (1957), quoted in *Academic Freedom: The Scholar's Place in Modern Society*, ed. Hans W. Baade and Robinson O. Everett (Dobbs Ferry: Oceana, 1964, reprinting an edition from the Duke University School of Law, 1963) 13, 26.

25. Baade and Everett, eds., *Academic Freedom* 36.

26. Homer P. Rainey, *The Tower and the Dome: A Free University Versus Political Control* (Boulder, Col.: Pruitt, 1971), is a markedly prejudiced account, but its documents include verbatim statements from his antagonists. Phi Beta Kappa and other academic associations, along with the AAUP (*AAUP Bulletin* 32 [1946]: 374–85) censured the board of regents. On this and other episodes of intimidation at the University of Texas see Ronnie Dugger, *Our Invaded Universities: Form, Reform, and New Starts* (New York: Norton, 1974).

27. *New York Times* 13 July 1997, Final National Edition: y17.

28. Madeleine J. Goodman, "The Review of Tenured Faculty at a Research University: Outcomes and Appraisals," *Review of Higher Education* 18.1 (1994): 83–94.

29. Donald Kennedy noted as closures "Archeology at Princeton, Architecture at Stanford, Demography at Berkeley, Library Science at Columbia, Organization and Management at Yale," *Daedalus* 122.4 (1993): 139. Geography had been closed elsewhere. Terry Belanger's rare books program at Columbia, banished to a wiser University of Virginia, was judged the best in the nation and had the best record of any program at Columbia in placing its graduates.

30. In an interview concerning the razing of two buildings of the Divinity School: Philip Langdon, "A Pattern of Destruction," *Preservation* 49.2 (1997): 15.

31. Christopher J. Lucas, *Crisis in the Academy: Rethinking Higher Education in America* (New York: St. Martin's, 1996) 11.

32. William H. Willimon and Thomas H. Naylor, *The Abandoned Generation: Rethinking Higher Education* (Grand Rapids, Mich.: Eerdmans, 1995) 101, citing Jon Marcus, "Tuitions Continue to Spiral," Associated Press 24 Sept. 1994.

33. P. J. Gumpert and B. Pusser, "A Case of Bureaucratic Accretion: Context and Consequences," *Journal of Higher Education* 66 (1995): 495, 500, 512–13.

34. *Chronicle of Higher Education* 24 Apr. 1991: A21; 9 Oct. 1991: A31.

35. Lynn Hunt, in *What's Happened to the Humanities?*, ed. Alvin Kernan (Princeton, N.J.: Princeton University Press, 1997) 21. Note also that these percentages include *all* faculty and begin with 1976; the reduction of full-time faculty had begun in 1971.

36. Martin Trow, "Comparative Reflections on Leadership in Higher Education," in *Higher Education in American Society*, ed. Philip G. Altbach, Robert O. Berdahl, and Patricia J. Gumport, 3rd ed. (Amherst, NY: Prometheus, 1994) 278–81, 283.

37. John Dale Russell, *The Finance of Higher Education*, rev. ed. (Chicago: University of Chicago Press, 1954) vii. Russell counted financial management a fifth responsibility after relationship to trustees, academic control, student personnel services, and effective public relations. As Robert and Jon Solomon conclude, "We have replaced educational thinking with corporate thinking and executive self-aggrandizement"—*Up the University: Re-Creating Higher Education in America* (Reading, Mass.: Addison-Wesley, 1993) 288.

38. Donald Kennedy, *Daedalus* 122.4 (1933): 147–48.

39. Jeff Jacoby, "How Not to Make College Affordable" 10 Feb. 1997, distributed nationally from the *Boston Globe* by the *New York Times* News Service. Jacoby's argument is that public subsidies to higher education encourage spending and thereby drive tuition upward.

SIX. NOW AND TOMORROW

1. Bruce Goldberg, *Why Schools Fail* (Washington: Cato, 1996) 43.

2. For one proposal of such service, as well as laboratory work for students of history and literature, see David H. Lempert et al., *Escape from the Ivory Tower: Student Adventures in Democratic Experiential Education* (San Francisco: Jossey-Bass, 1996). In escape to the lab, students would "see detail and find subtlety and pattern through experiences of seeing, recording, and interpreting" (105). Robert and Jon Solomon, in *Up the University: Recreating Higher Education in America* (Reading, Mass.: Addison-Wesley, 1993), find hope for reduction of research and consequent democratic service only in state universities and community colleges, but students in private universities and colleges have formed groups to do voluntarily what deans and faculties could require.

3. John Holdren and E. D. Hirsch Jr., eds., *Books to Build On: A Grade-by-Grade Resource Guide for Parents and Teachers* (New York: Delta, 1996).

4. Allan Bloom, *The Closing of the American Mind* (New York: Simon & Schuster, 1987) 340.

5. George Wilson Pierson, *Yale College: An Educational History, 1871–1921* (New Haven: Yale University Press, 1952) 202–11. For Eliot's travail at Harvard, see Samuel Eliot Morison, *Three Centuries of Harvard, 1636–1936* (Cambridge: Harvard University Press, 1936) xliv-xlvii.

6. John R. Thelin, *Higher Education and Its Useful Past: Applied History in Research and Planning* (Cambridge, Mass.: Schenkman, 1982) 158, 160.

7. Jan Sinnott and Lynn Johnson, *Reinventing the University: A Radical Proposal for a Problem-Focused University* (Norwood, N.J.: Ablex, 1996) 28.

8. "For College Classroom Blackboards, an Electronic Form," *New York Times* 8 Apr. 1997, Education Life 7, 12.

9. "The Blessed Damozel" is one cyberspace threat cited in the Association of American Colleges' Winter 1993 number of *Liberal Education* on "The Future of the Book."

10. These are not teaching systems but learning systems that produce (under tutelage) an "active, empowered reader," according to George P. Landow, *Hypertext: The Convergence of Contemporary Critical Theory and Technology* (Baltimore, Md.: Johns Hopkins University Press, 1992) 120.

11. Marvin W. Peterson et al., *Planning and Management for a Changing Environment: A Handbook on Redesigning Postsecondary Institutions* (San Francisco: Jossey-Bass, 1997) 432.

12. Louie Crew, "Back to the Future," in *English as a Discipline; or, Is There a Plot in This Play?*, ed. James C. Raymond (Tuscaloosa: University of Alabama Press, 1996) 44–61.

13. "How the Academic Profession Is Changing," *Daedalus* 126.4 (1997): 14–16.

14. "Uncertainties in the Changing Academic Profession," Daedalus 126.4 (1997): 76–7.

15. Paul Woodring, *The Higher Learning in America: A Reassessment* (New York: McGraw-Hill, 1968) 176, 177.

16. Interview, Robert Lenzner and Stephen S. Johnson, "Seeing Things as They Really Are," *Forbes*, 10 March 1997: 127.

17. Morison, *Three Centuries of Harvard* 90.

SEVEN. TEACHING: WHAT AND HOW

1. Giovanni della Casa, *Galateo*, trans. Robert Peterson (1576), ed. J. E. Spingarn (1914), here from *Another World Than This*, compiled by V. Sackville-West and Harold Nicolson (London: Michael Joseph, 1945) 16.

2. Francis Oakley, in *What's Happened to the Humanities?*, ed. Alvin Kernan (Princeton, N.J.: Princeton University Press, 1997) 72.

3. A similar proposal is among the recommendations by Carl R. Lovitt and Art Young, "Rethinking Genre in the First-Year Composition Course: Helping Student Writers Get Things Done,"in *Profession 1997* (New York: Modern Language Association of America, 1997) 113–25.

4. The course is central to Elizabeth Chiseri-Strater, *Academic Literacies: The Public and Private Discourse of University Students* (Portsmouth, N.H.: Boynton/Cook/Heinemann, 1991).

5. *Webster's Dictionary of Synonyms* (Springfield, Mass., Merriam-Webster, 1942) 442.

6. For two of many available examples, see Margery Savin, in Kernan, ed., *What's Happened to the Humanities?* 98–100.

7. Logic and rhetoric, a required seminar in composition, remains with foreign languages and sciences in the prescribed core. Mathematics is a prerequisite for admission; the list of courses approved to meet the science requirement includes calculus. My interest here is not in the Columbia College solution to requirements but in the successful preservation there of a commonalty not effaced by electives.

8. In *Columbia Literary History of the United States*, ed. Emory Elliott, et al. (New York: Columbia University Press, 1988) 731.

9. David Denby, *Great Books* (New York: Simon & Schuster, 1996) 461.

10. Charles Bernstein, "A Blow Is Like an Instrument," *Daedalus* 126.4 (1997): 178, 181.

11. George Washington, "Last Will and Testament," in *Writings*, ed. John Rhodehamel (New York: Library of America, 1997) 1026. In his own draft for his first inaugural, Washington urged members of Congress "to use your best endeavours to improve the education and manners of a people; to accelerate the progress of arts & Sciences; to patronize works of genius; to confer rewards for inventions of utility; and to cherish institutions favourable to humanity" (715).

12. Gerald Graff, *Beyond the Culture Wars: How Teaching the Conflicts Can Revitalize American Education* (New York: Norton, 1992) 173.

13. E. D. Hirsch Jr., *Cultural Literacy: What Every American Needs to Know* (Boston: Houghton Mifflin, 1987).

14. On the turmoil and compromises at Stanford since abandonment of the required "Western Civilization" in 1973, see the brief account by Henry Rosovsky and Inge-Lise Ameer in *Universities and Their Leadership*, ed. William G. Bowen and Harold T. Shapiro (Princeton, N.J.: Princeton University Press, 1998) 130–43.

15. "Homer's Women," *New Yorker* 27 Jan 1997: 74. I quote Pope's Iliad 5.668–69. In keeping with its own argument, Wills's review of Fales's translation can be used to "prove" that Fales and Wills read a different Chapman's Homer from the "wide expanse" that inspired Keats.

16. "Evolution and Revolution: Change in the Literary Humanities, 1968–1995," in Kernan, ed., *What's Happened to the Humanities?* 87 and n. 9.

17. Stephen Greenblatt and Giles Gunn, *Redrawing the Boundaries: The Transformation of English and American Literary Studies* (New York: Modern Language Association, 1992) 5. From listening to representatives of all chronological periods and several areas, they saw the question of the 1990s as "What constitutes literary interest in the first place?" with the problem "to resituate all the interrogatory operations of criticism within new constellations of force and tension" (9, 10).

18. Robert Hodge, *Literature as Discourse: Textual Strategies in English and History* (Baltimore, Md.: Johns Hopkins University Press, 1990).

19. Louis Menand, ed., *The Future of Academic Freedom* (Chicago: University of Chicago Press, 1996) 11.

20. Page Smith, *Killing the Spirit: Higher Education in America* (New York: Viking, 1990) 7.

21. Vaclav Havel, "Faith in the World," *Civilization* 5.2 (1998): 53.

22. "Ethics and Ethnicity," *Bulletin of the American Academy of Arts and Sciences* 51.1 (1997): 47. Gates describes "the internal diversity" as a collective identity within each individual.

APPENDIX

1. Quoted in Avrel Seale, "Can Ford Make UT More Aerodynamic?" *Texas Alcalde* 86.3 (1998): 21. The Ford Motor Company has adopted the University of Texas, Michigan State, Ohio State, Wayne State, and Howard, as IBM adopted the University of Wisconsin at Madison, Motorola adopted Purdue, and Xerox adopted Carnegie-Mellon, among twenty corporations adopting forty-four universities. "To date, Ford has donated approximately $400,000 of in-kind expenses like room, meal, and travel for UT administrators to come to Dearborn and learn."

2. *Columbia University Record*, 21 May 1997: 2.

3. "Boulder Dam," *Abe Burrows Sings?* (Columbia Records, 1950).

4. Karen Hess Rogers, "Then and Now," *The Flyleaf* 47.3 (1997): 15.

5. The information for each institution is taken from directories, bulletins, and catalogues. The margin of error will be less than that in objective polls.

INDEX